" The mind-forg'd manacles I hear "

William Blake

FOR TRACEY

BLACK✗CHARITY™

BAL SPEER

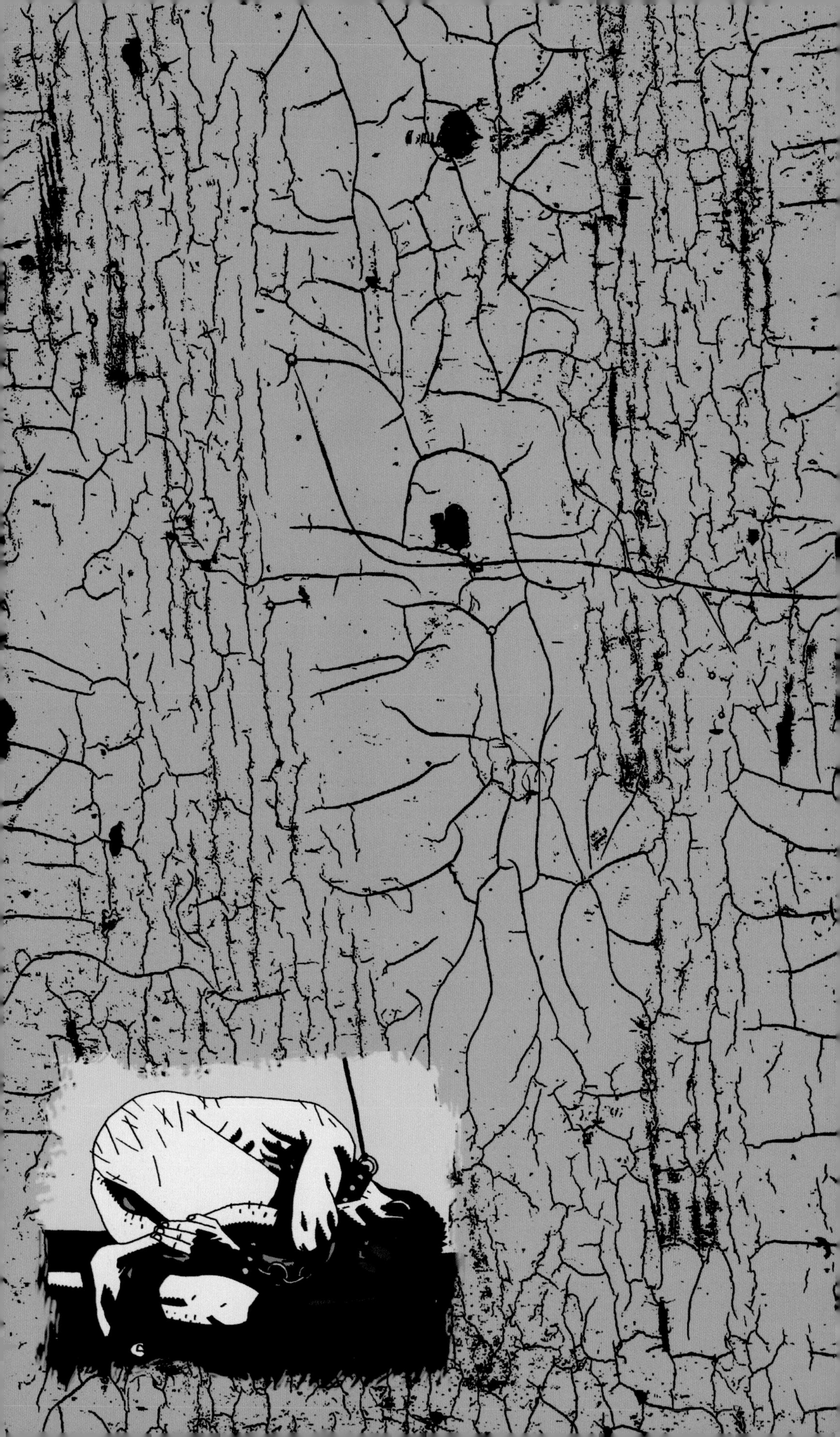

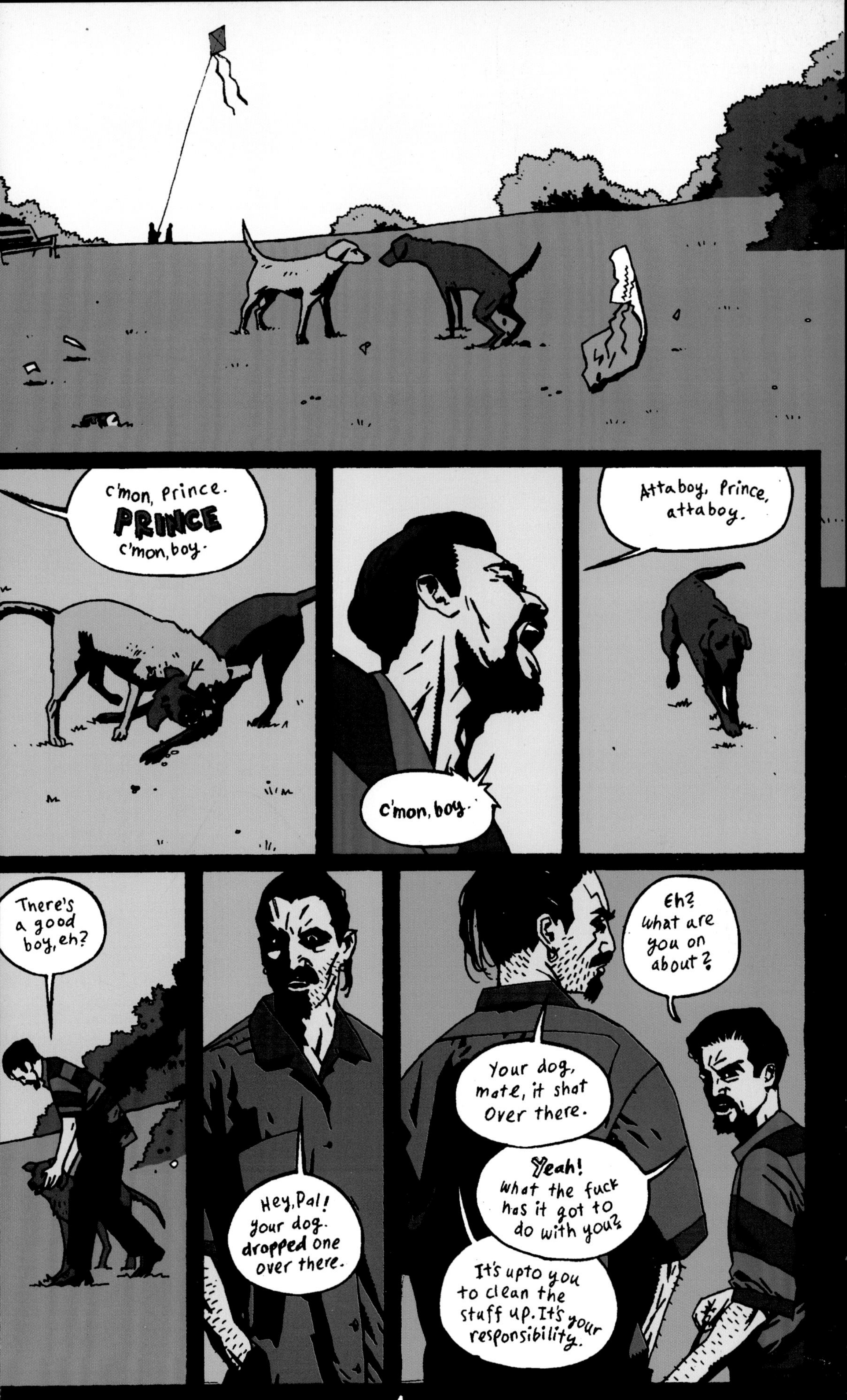
c'mon, Prince.
PRINCE
c'mon, boy.
C'mon, boy.
Attaboy, Prince, attaboy.
There's a good boy, eh?
Hey, Pal! your dog. dropped one over there.
Eh? what are you on about?
Your dog, mate, it shat over there.
Yeah! what the fuck has it got to do with you?
It's upto you to clean the stuff up. It's your responsibility.

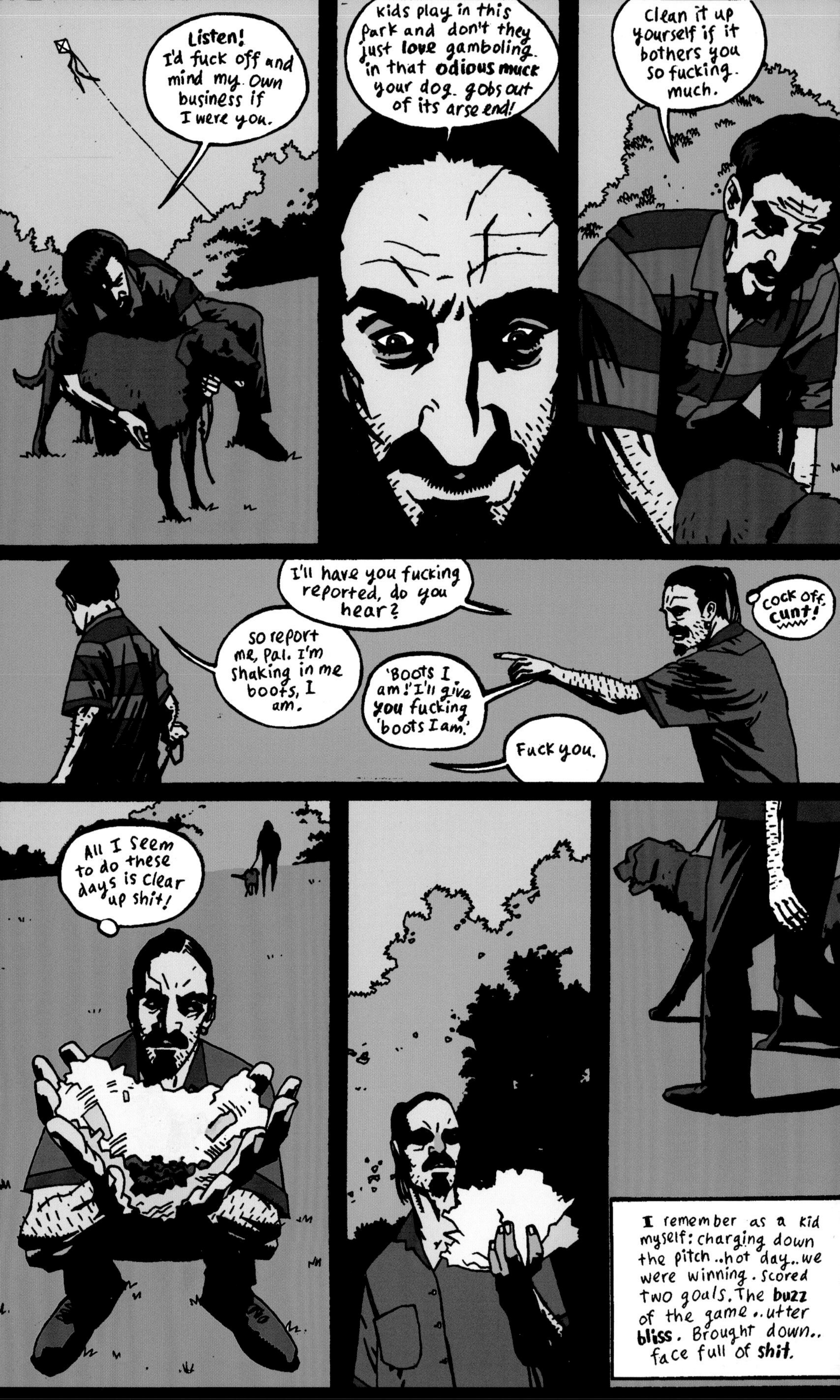
Listen! I'd fuck off and mind my own business if I were you.
kids play in this park and don't they just love gamboling in that odious muck your dog gobs out of its arse end!
Clean it up yourself if it bothers you so fucking much.
I'll have you fucking reported, do you hear?
so report me, pal. I'm shaking in me boots, I am.
cock off, cunt!
'Boots I am!' I'll give you fucking 'boots I am.'
Fuck you.
All I seem to do these days is clear up shit!
I remember as a kid myself: charging down the pitch .. hot day .. we were winning. Scored two goals. The buzz of the game .. utter bliss. Brought down .. face full of shit.

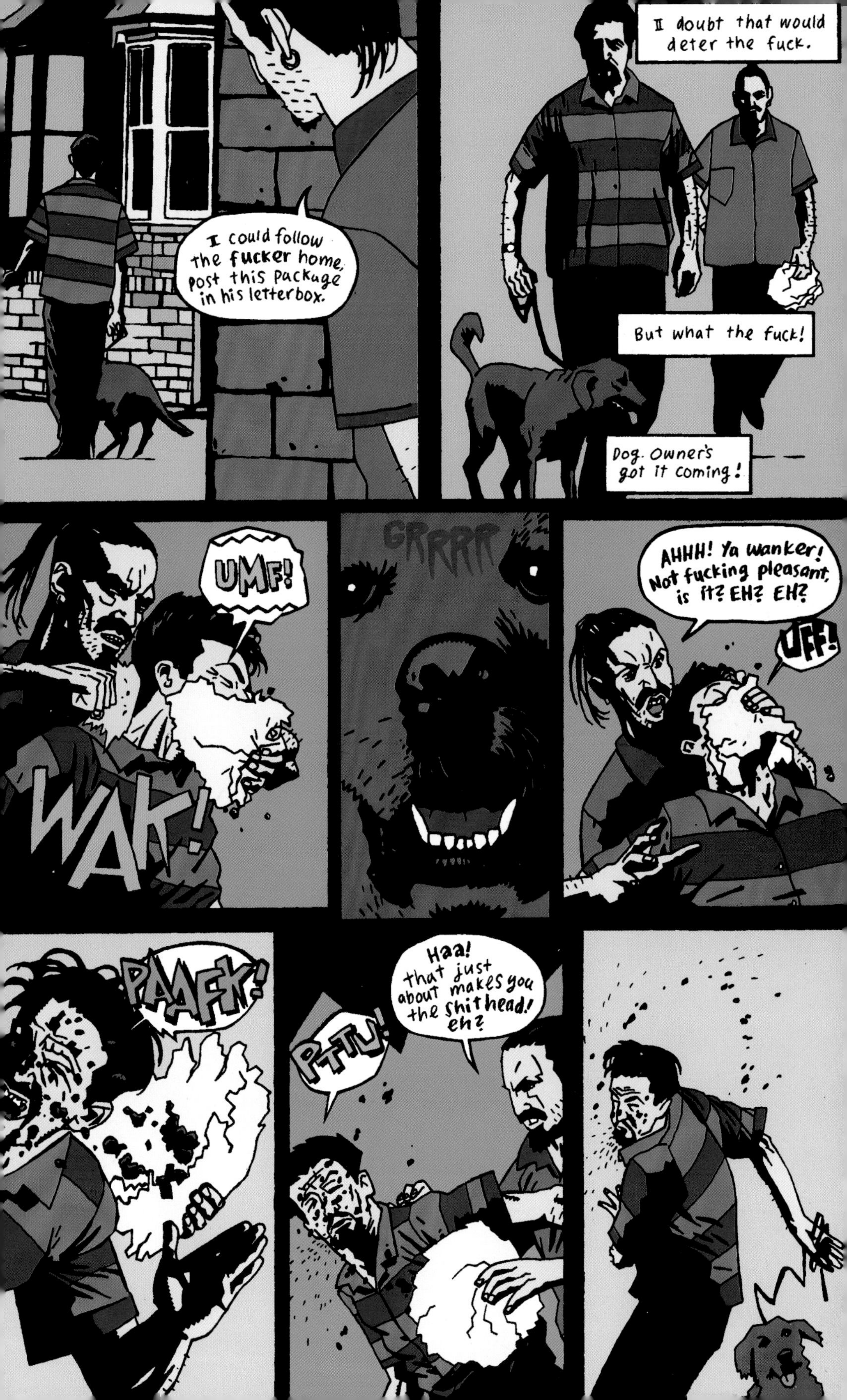
I could follow the fucker home, post this package in his letterbox.
I doubt that would deter the fuck.
But what the fuck!
Dog. Owner's got it coming!
UMF!
WAK!
GRRRR
AHHH! Ya wanker! Not fucking pleasant, is it? EH? EH?
UFF!
PAAFK!
PTTU!
Haa! that just about makes you the shithead! eh?

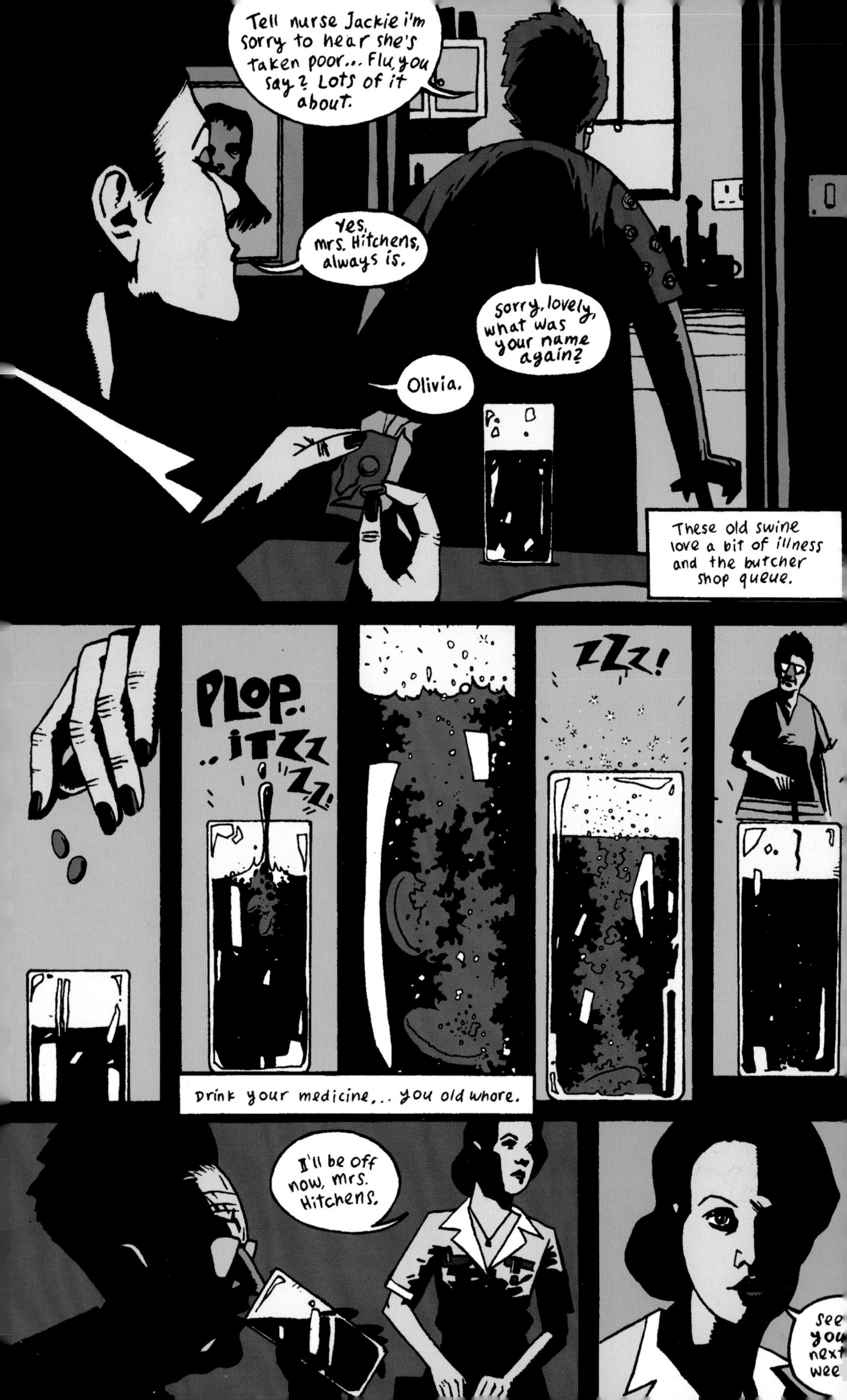

Tell nurse Jackie i'm sorry to hear she's taken poor... Flu, you say? Lots of it about.
Yes, mrs. Hitchens, always is.
Sorry, lovely, what was your name again?
Olivia.
These old swine love a bit of illness and the butcher shop queue.
PLOP.. ..iTZZ ZZ!
ZZZ!
Drink your medicine... you old whore.
I'll be off now, mrs. Hitchens.

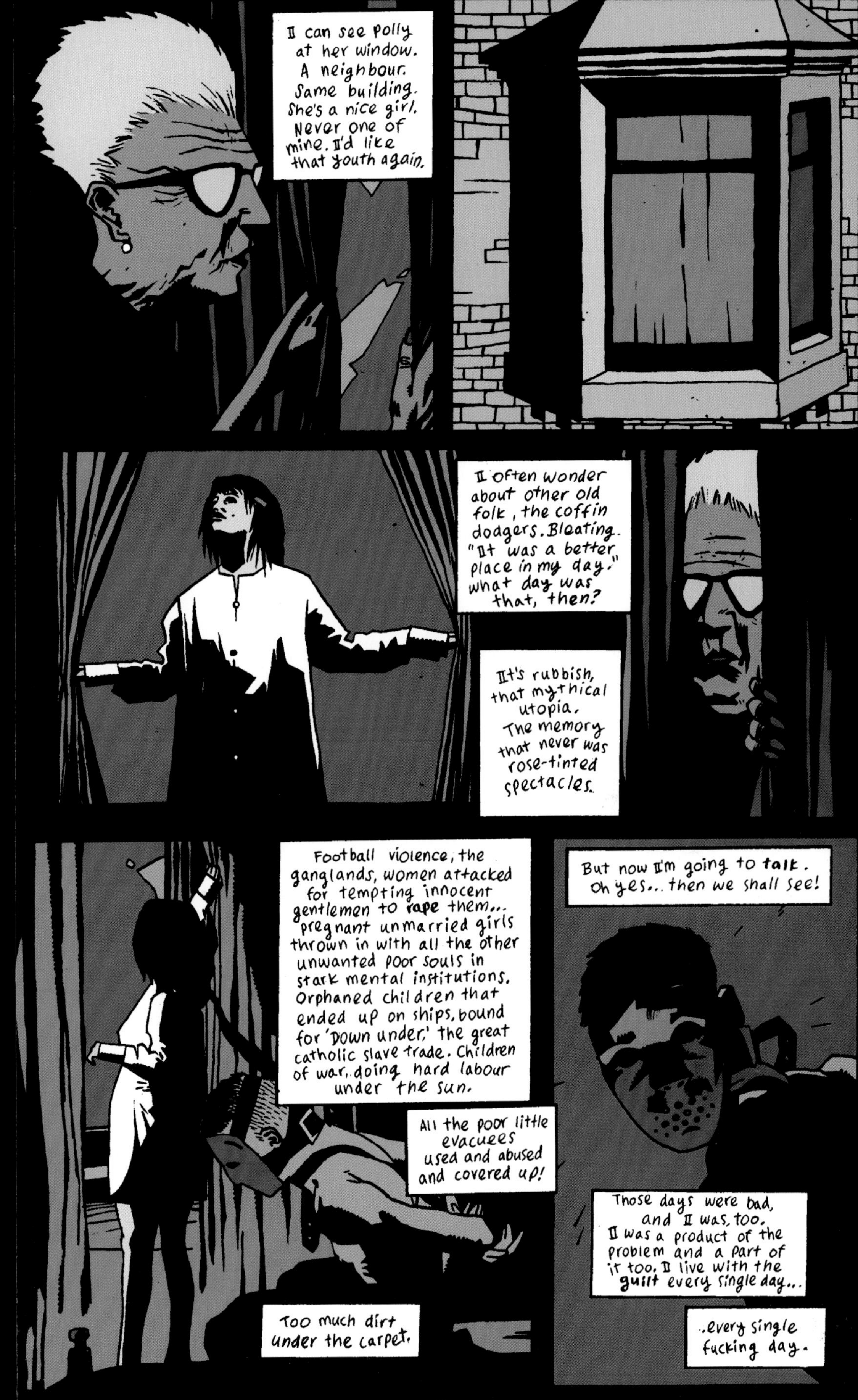
I can see Polly at her window. A neighbour. Same building. She's a nice girl. Never one of mine. I'd like that youth again.
I often wonder about other old folk, the coffin dodgers. Bleating. "It was a better place in my day." What day was that, then?
It's rubbish, that mythical utopia. The memory that never was rose-tinted spectacles.
Football violence, the ganglands, women attacked for tempting innocent gentlemen to **rape** them... pregnant unmarried girls thrown in with all the other unwanted poor souls in stark mental institutions. Orphaned children that ended up on ships, bound for 'Down under,' the great catholic slave trade. Children of war, doing hard labour under the sun.
All the poor little evacuees used and abused and covered up!
Too much dirt under the carpet.
But now I'm going to **talk**. Oh yes... then we shall see!
Those days were bad, and I was, too. I was a product of the problem and a part of it too. I live with the **guilt** every single day...
..every single fucking day.

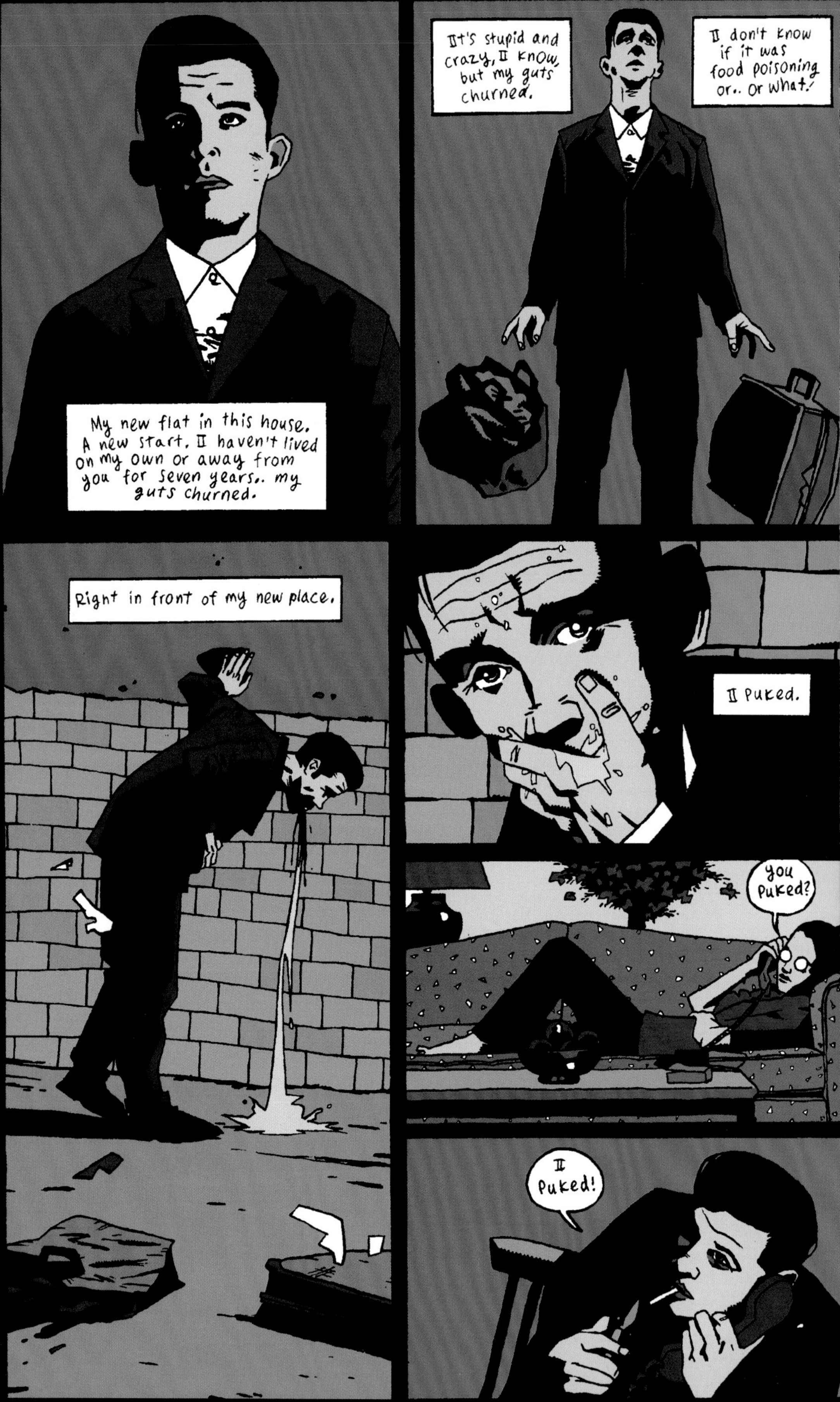
My new flat in this house. A new start. I haven't lived on my own or away from you for seven years.. my guts churned.
It's stupid and crazy, I know, but my guts churned.
I don't know if it was food poisoning or.. or what.
Right in front of my new place.
I puked.
you puked?
I puked!

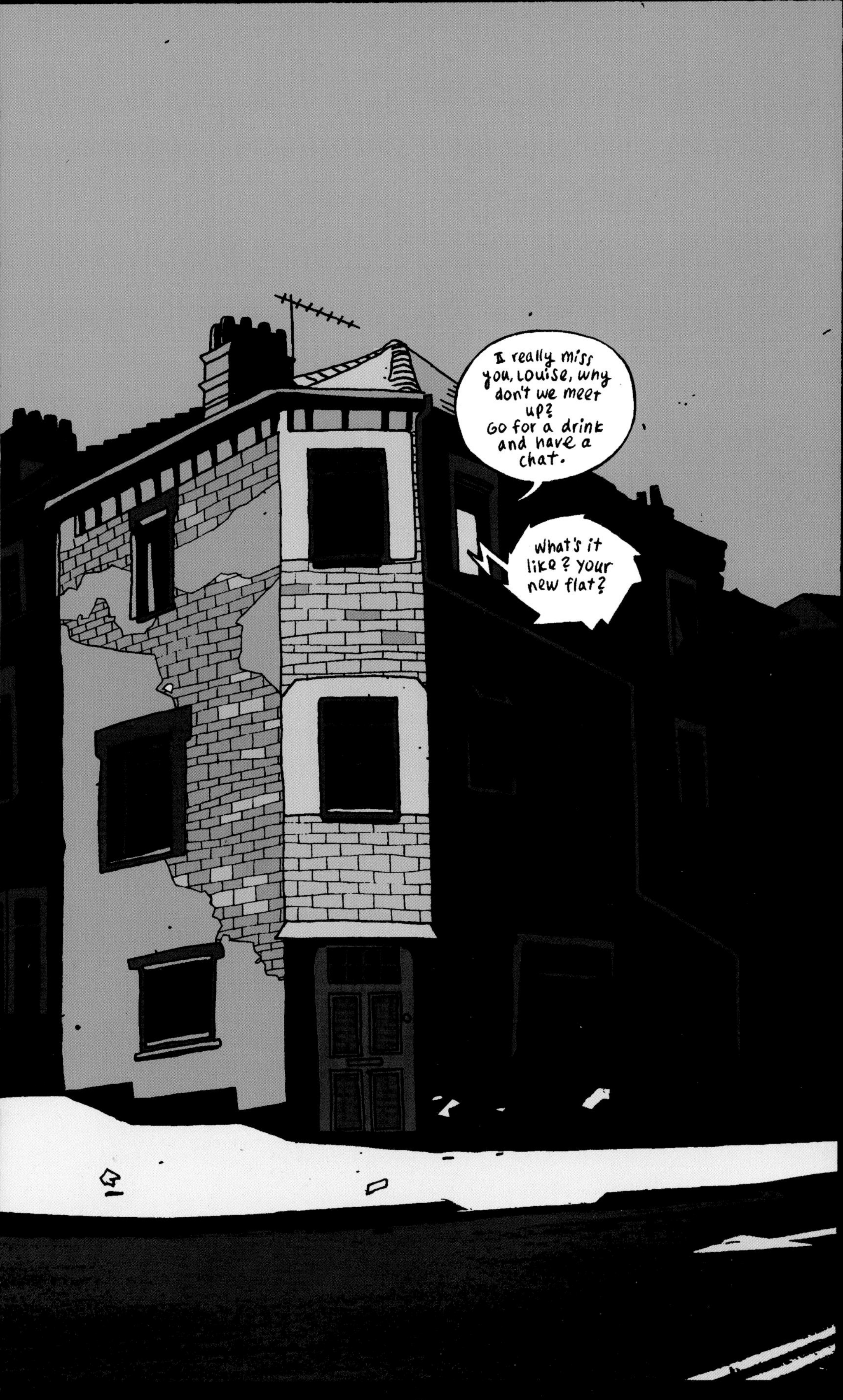
I really miss you, Louise, why don't we meet up? Go for a drink and have a chat.
What's it like? your new flat?

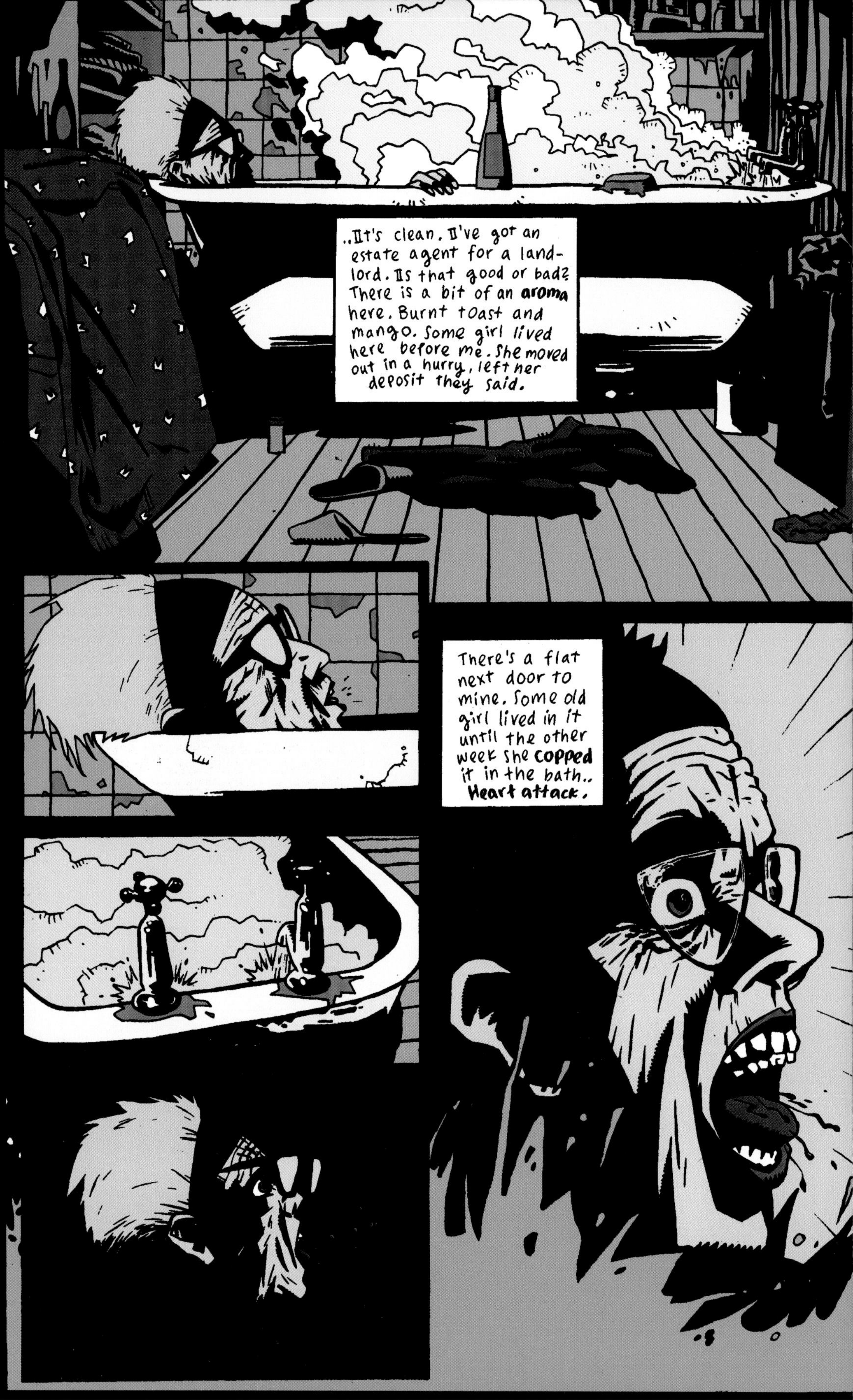
..It's clean. I've got an estate agent for a land-lord. Is that good or bad? There is a bit of an aroma here. Burnt toast and mango. Some girl lived here before me. She moved out in a hurry, left her deposit they said.
There's a flat next door to mine. Some old girl lived in it until the other week she copped it in the bath.. Heart attack.

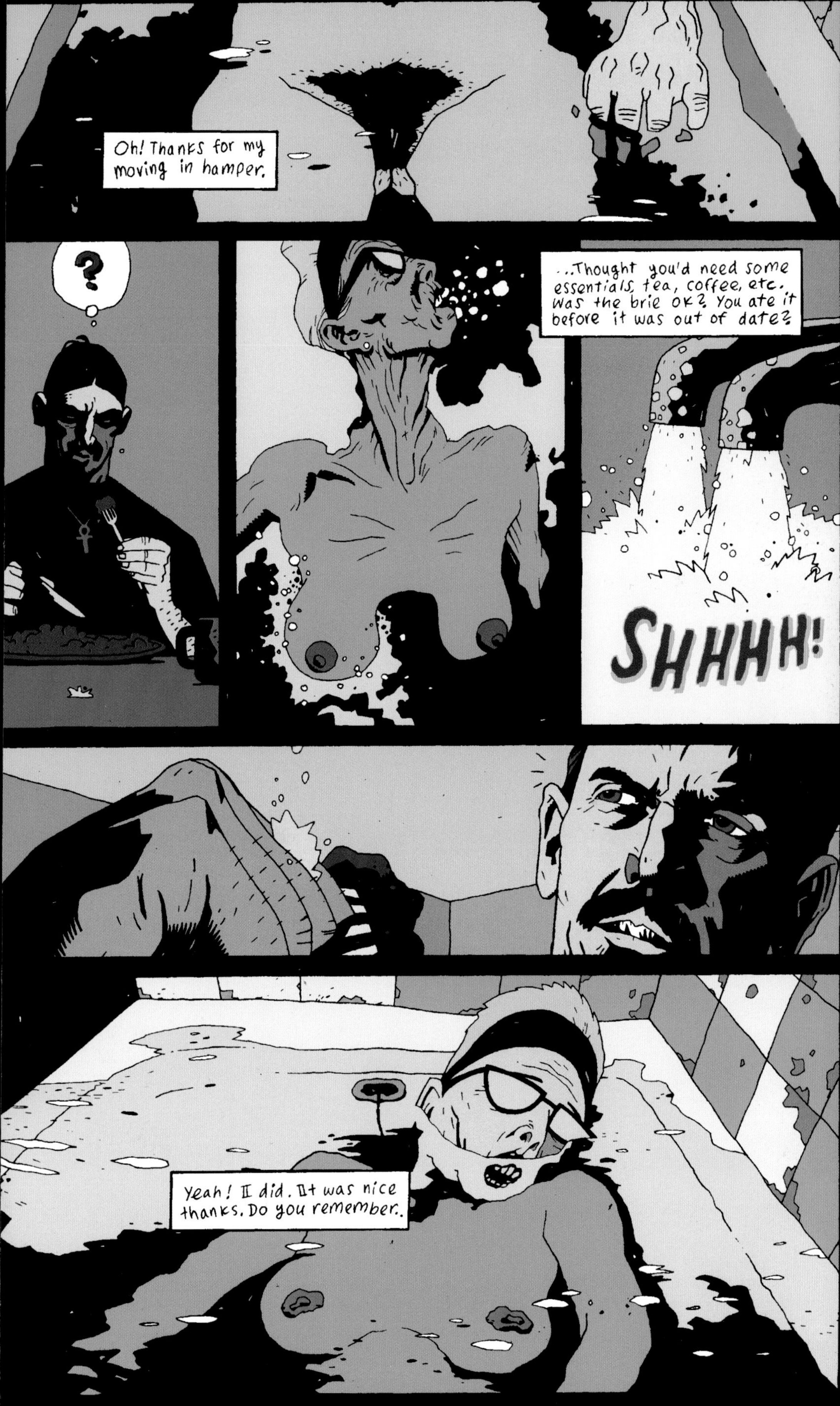
Oh! Thanks for my moving in hamper.
?
..Thought you'd need some essentials, tea, coffee, etc. Was the brie OK? You ate it before it was out of date?
SHHHH!
Yeah! I did. It was nice thanks. Do you remember..

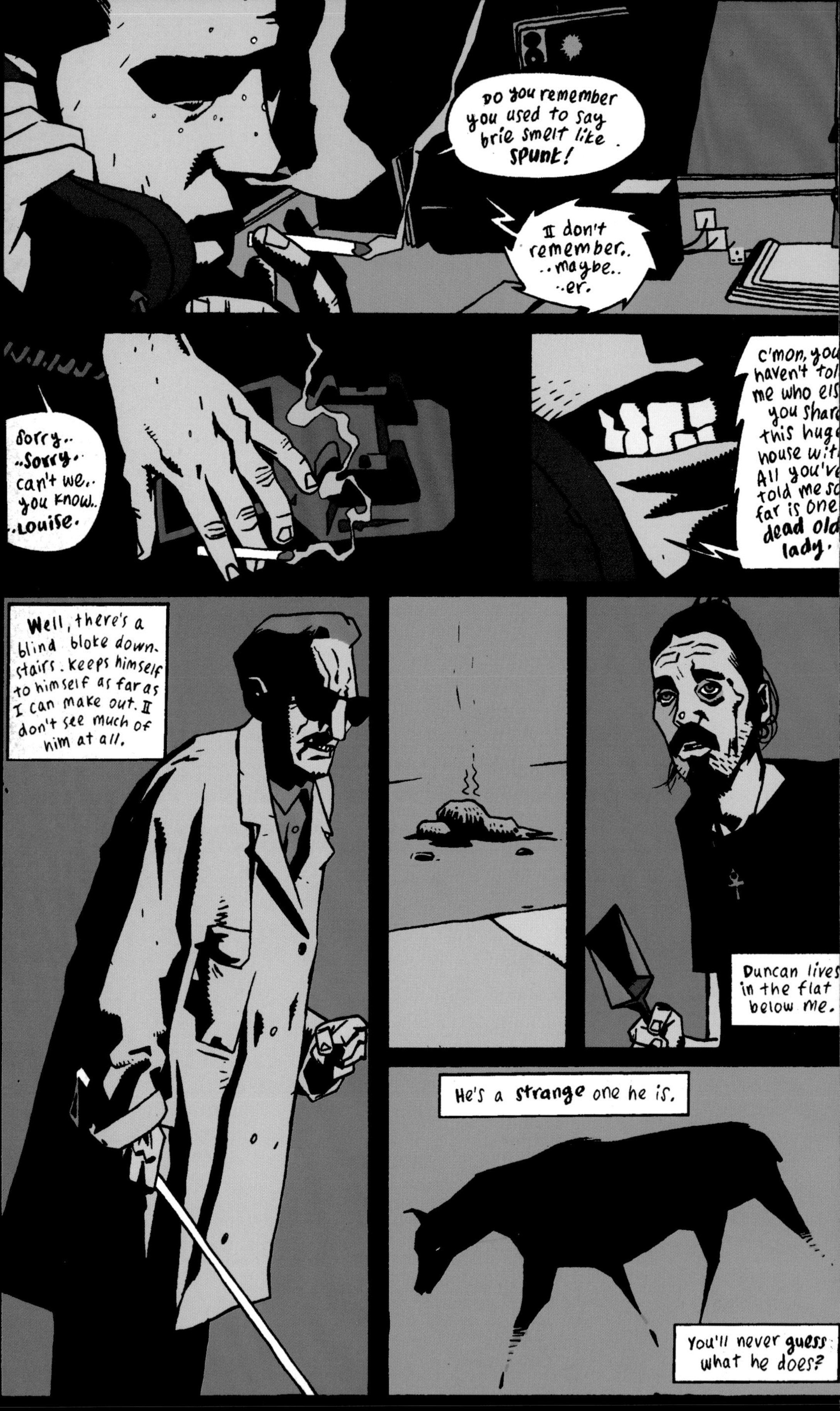
Do you remember you used to say brie smelt like **spunk**!
I don't remember.. ..maybe.. ..er.
Sorry.. ..**Sorry**.. can't we.. you know.. ..**Louise**.
c'mon, you haven't tol me who els you shar this hug house wit All you've told me so far is one **dead old lady**.
Well, there's a blind bloke down-stairs. Keeps himself to himself as far as I can make out. I don't see much of him at all.
Duncan lives in the flat below me.
He's a **strange** one he is.
You'll never **guess** what he does?

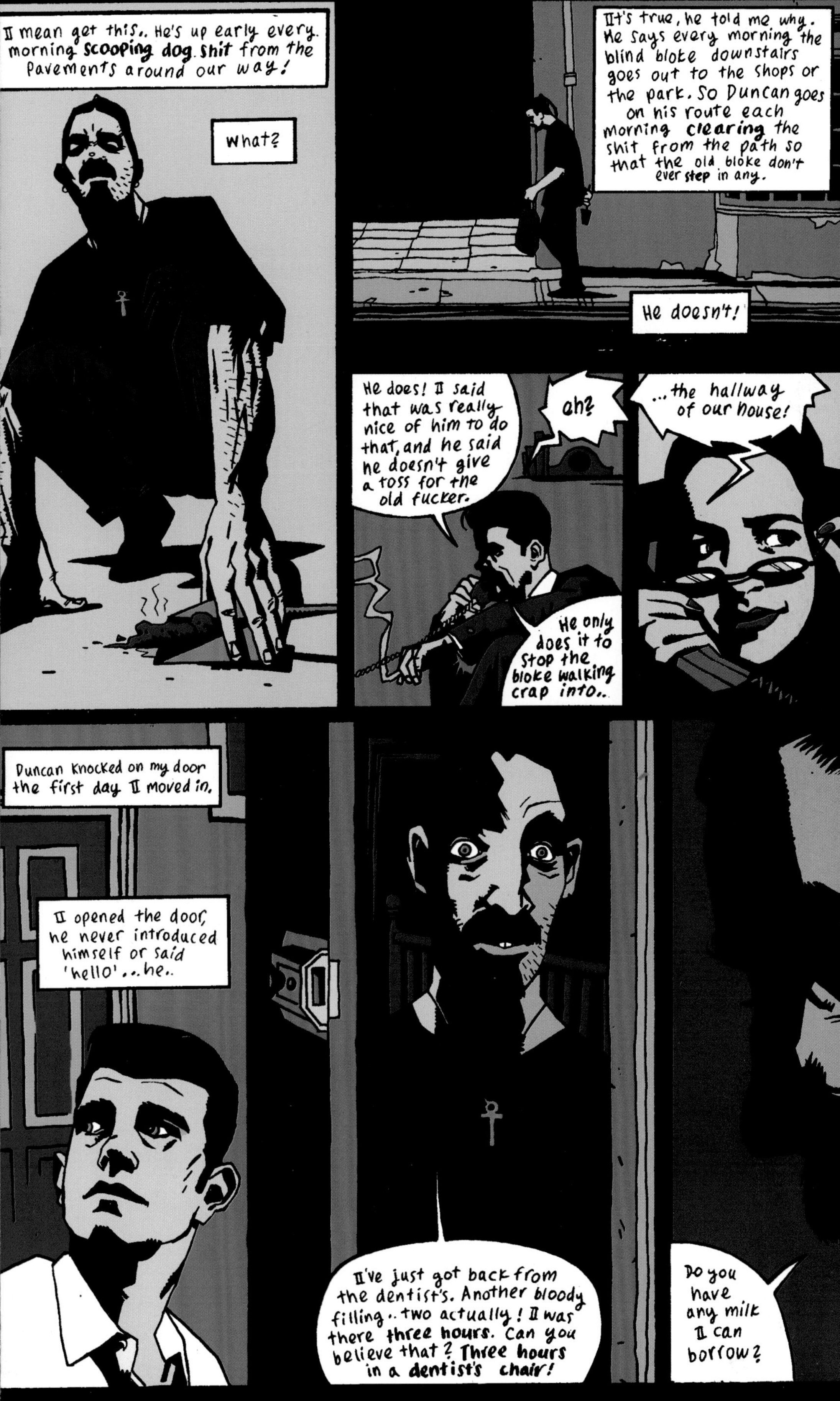

I mean get this.. He's up early every morning scooping dog shit from the pavements around our way!
What?
It's true, he told me why. He says every morning the blind bloke downstairs goes out to the shops or the park. So Duncan goes on his route each morning clearing the shit from the path so that the old bloke don't ever step in any.
He doesn't!
He does! I said that was really nice of him to do that, and he said he doesn't give a toss for the old fucker.
oh?
He only does it to stop the bloke walking crap into..
...the hallway of our house!
Duncan knocked on my door the first day I moved in.
I opened the door, he never introduced himself or said 'hello'...he..
I've just got back from the dentist's. Another bloody filling.. two actually! I was there three hours. Can you believe that? Three hours in a dentist's chair!
Do you have any milk I can borrow?

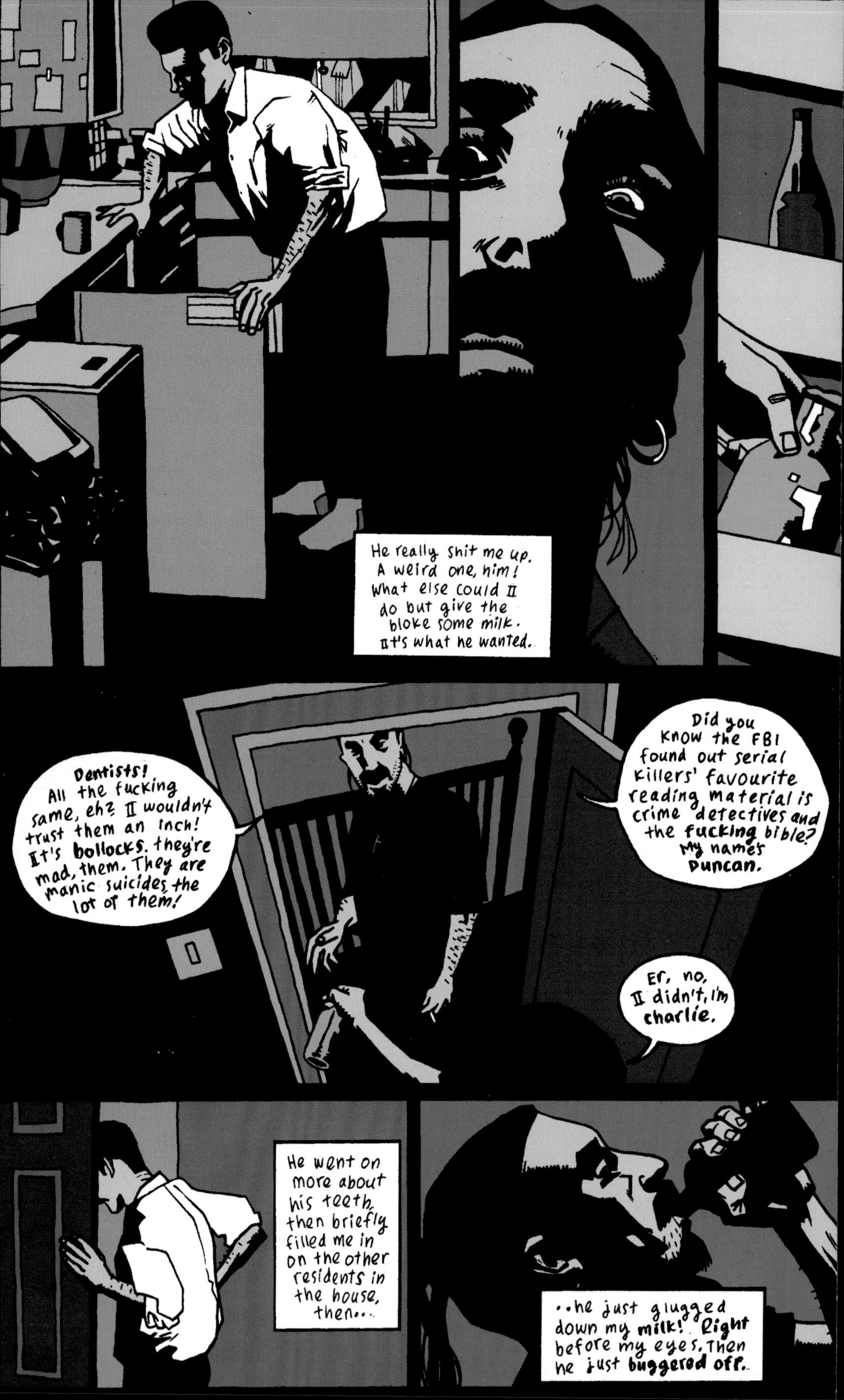
He really shit me up. A weird one, him! What else could I do but give the bloke some milk. It's what he wanted.
Dentists! All the fucking same, eh? I wouldn't trust them an inch! It's bollocks. they're mad, them. They are manic suicides, the lot of them!
Did you know the FBI found out serial killers' favourite reading material is crime detectives and the fucking bible? My name's Duncan.
Er, no, I didn't, I'm Charlie.
He went on more about his teeth, then briefly filled me in on the other residents in the house, then...
..he just glugged down my milk! Right before my eyes. Then he just buggered off..

What's she like?

I haven't seen her yet.

And there's this girl, she lives alone in the flat across from me.

I don't know.

Duncan says she has her own business. But he never said what it is. He never told me what he did either.

Actually, I had seen her. She was **gorgeous**, she had something about her... a **mystique!**

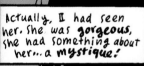

Gotta go, Charlie, my program's starting.

Louise.

Louise.

I'm kind of glad I met Duncan. I think one should always have a nutter as a casual acquaintance.

Where did I go wrong, Louise? Where **the fuck** did I go **wrong?**

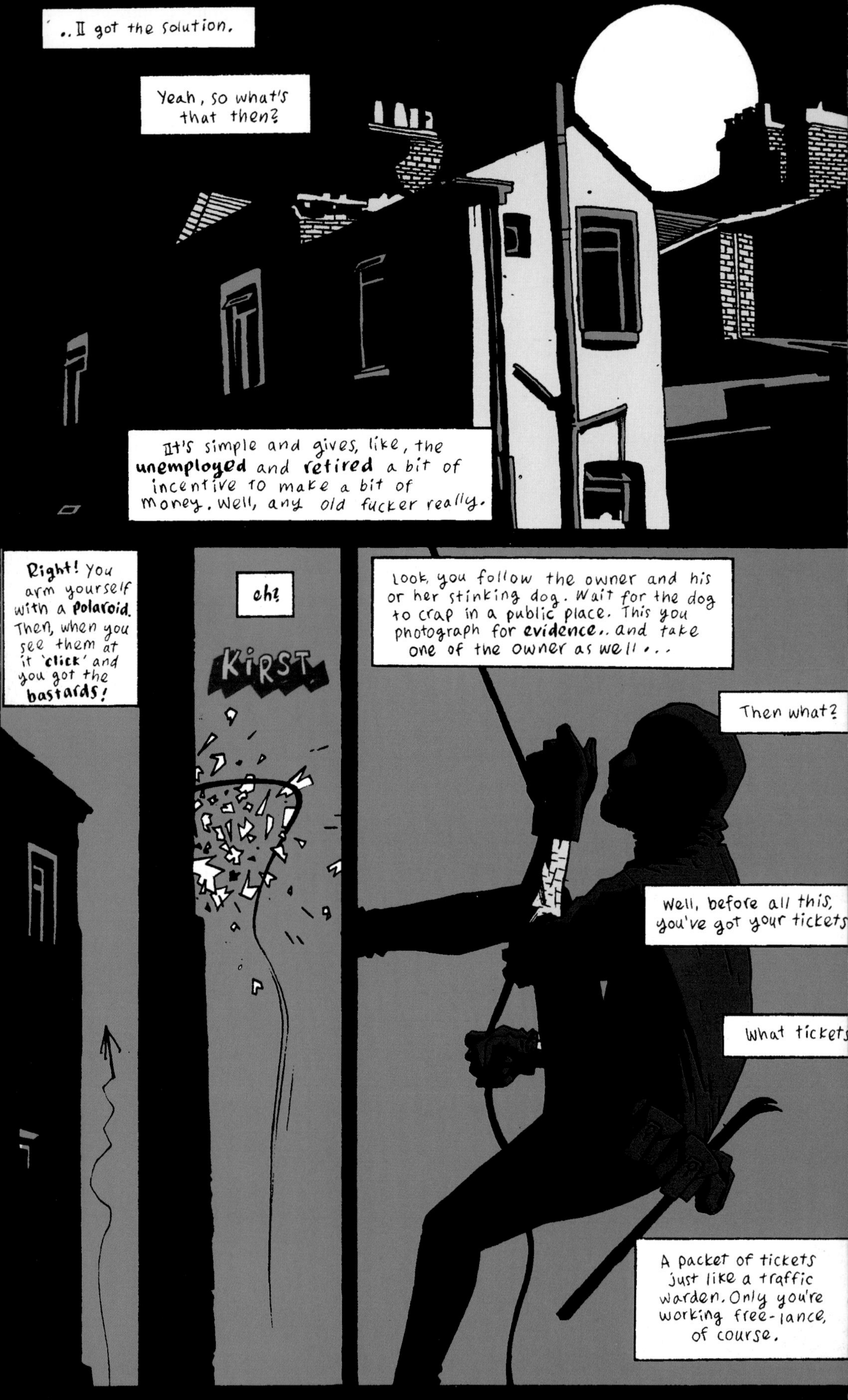
..I got the solution.
Yeah, so what's that then?
It's simple and gives, like, the **unemployed** and **retired** a bit of incentive to make a bit of money. Well, any old fucker really.
Right! You arm yourself with a **Polaroid**. Then, when you see them at it **'click'** and you got the **bastards!**
eh?
KIRST
Look, you follow the owner and his or her stinking dog. Wait for the dog to crap in a public place. This you photograph for **evidence**.. and take one of the owner as well...
Then what?
Well, before all this, you've got your tickets
What tickets
A packet of tickets just like a traffic warden. Only you're working free-lance, of course.

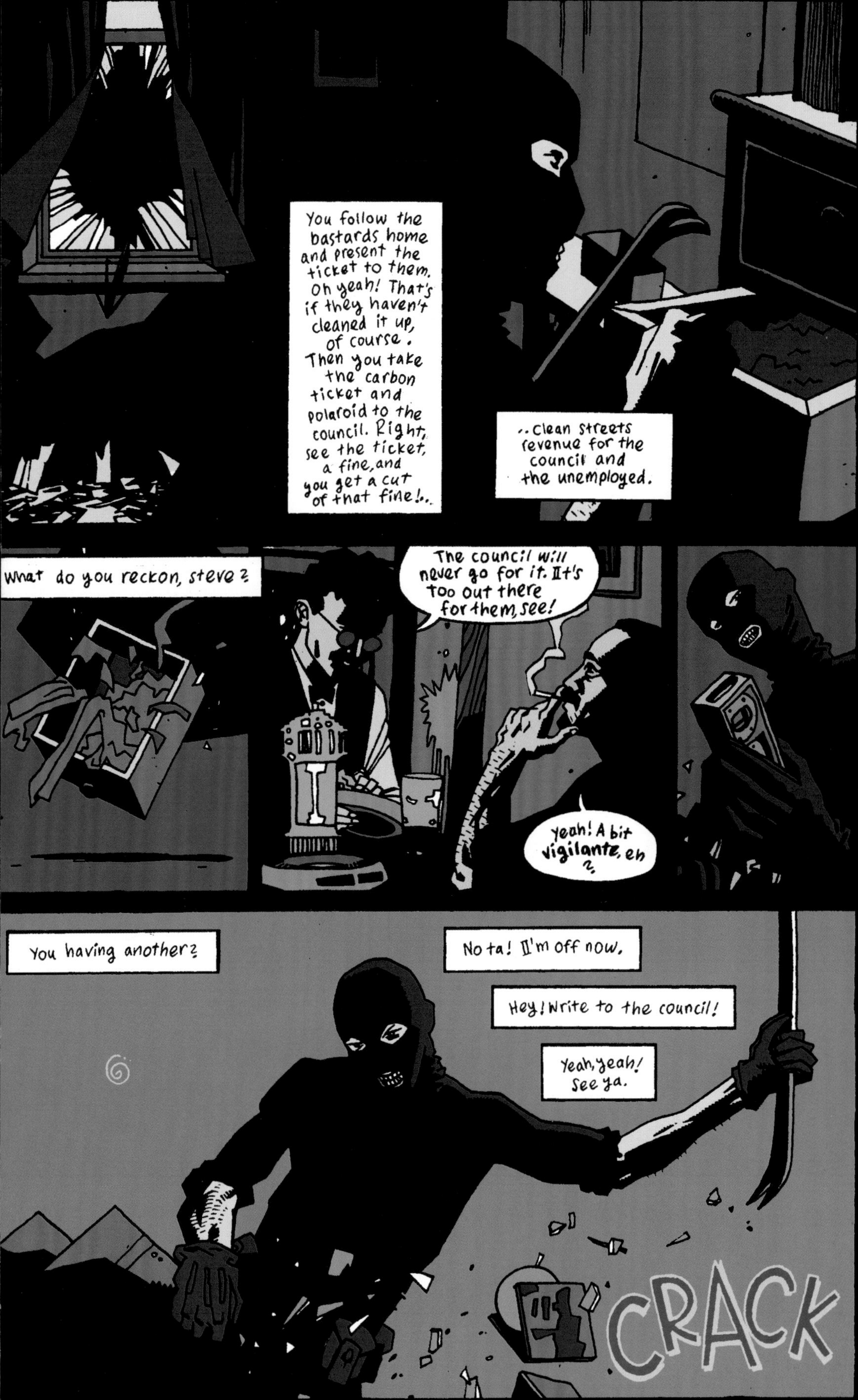
You follow the bastards home and present the ticket to them. Oh yeah! That's if they haven't cleaned it up, of course. Then you take the carbon ticket and polaroid to the council. Right, see the ticket, a fine, and you get a cut of that fine!..
..Clean streets revenue for the council and the unemployed.
What do you reckon, steve?
The council will never go for it. It's too out there for them, see!
yeah! A bit vigilante, eh?
You having another?
No ta! I'm off now.
Hey! Write to the council!
Yeah, yeah! See ya.
CRACK

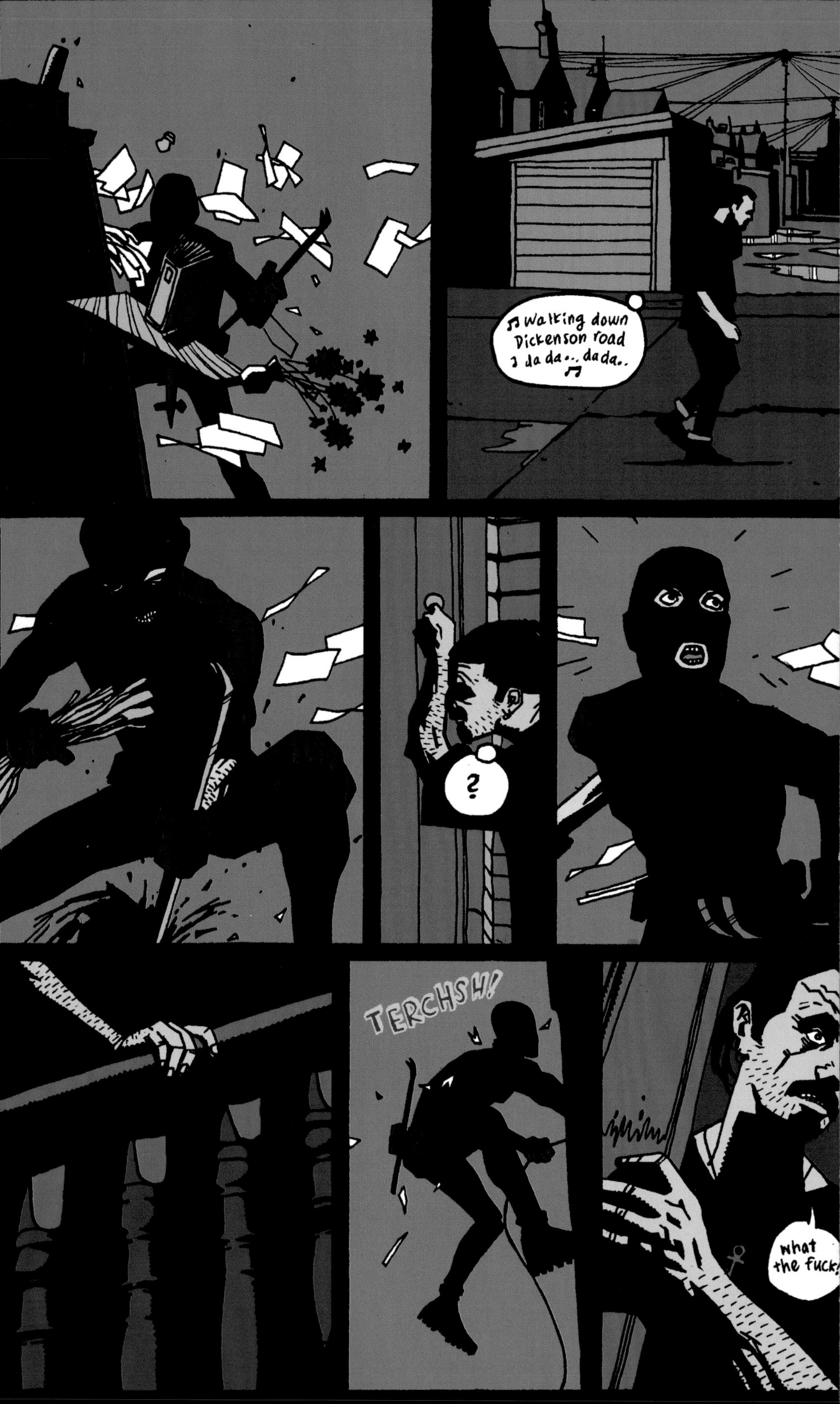
♫ walking down Dickenson road ♪ da da.., da da..
?
TERCHSH!
what the fuck!

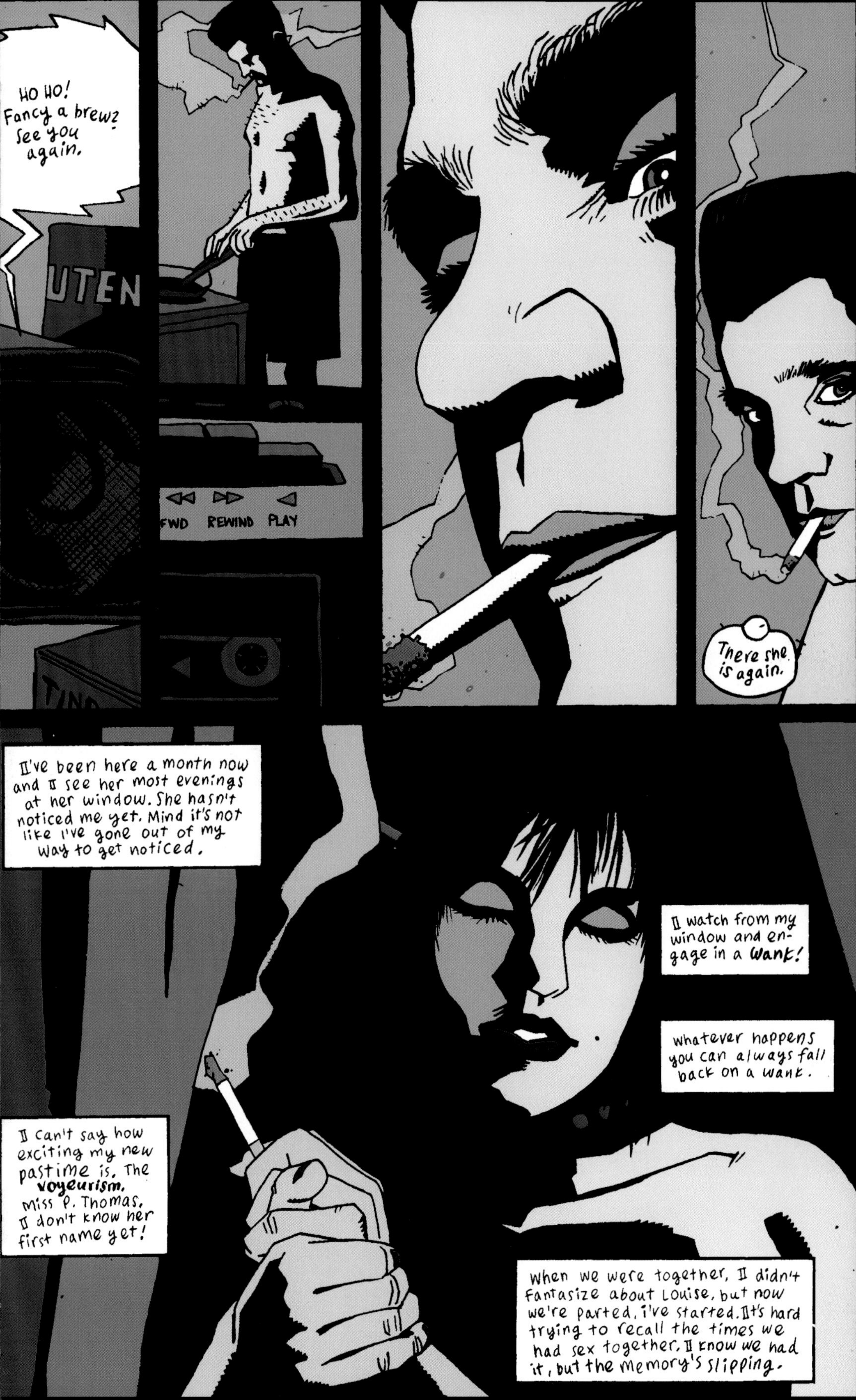
HO HO! Fancy a brew? See you again.
UTEN
FWD REWIND PLAY
There she is again.
I've been here a month now and I see her most evenings at her window. She hasn't noticed me yet. Mind it's not like I've gone out of my way to get noticed.
I watch from my window and engage in a wank!
Whatever happens you can always fall back on a wank.
I can't say how exciting my new pastime is. The voyeurism. Miss P. Thomas. I don't know her first name yet!
When we were together, I didn't fantasize about Louise, but now we're parted, I've started. It's hard trying to recall the times we had sex together. I know we had it, but the memory's slipping.

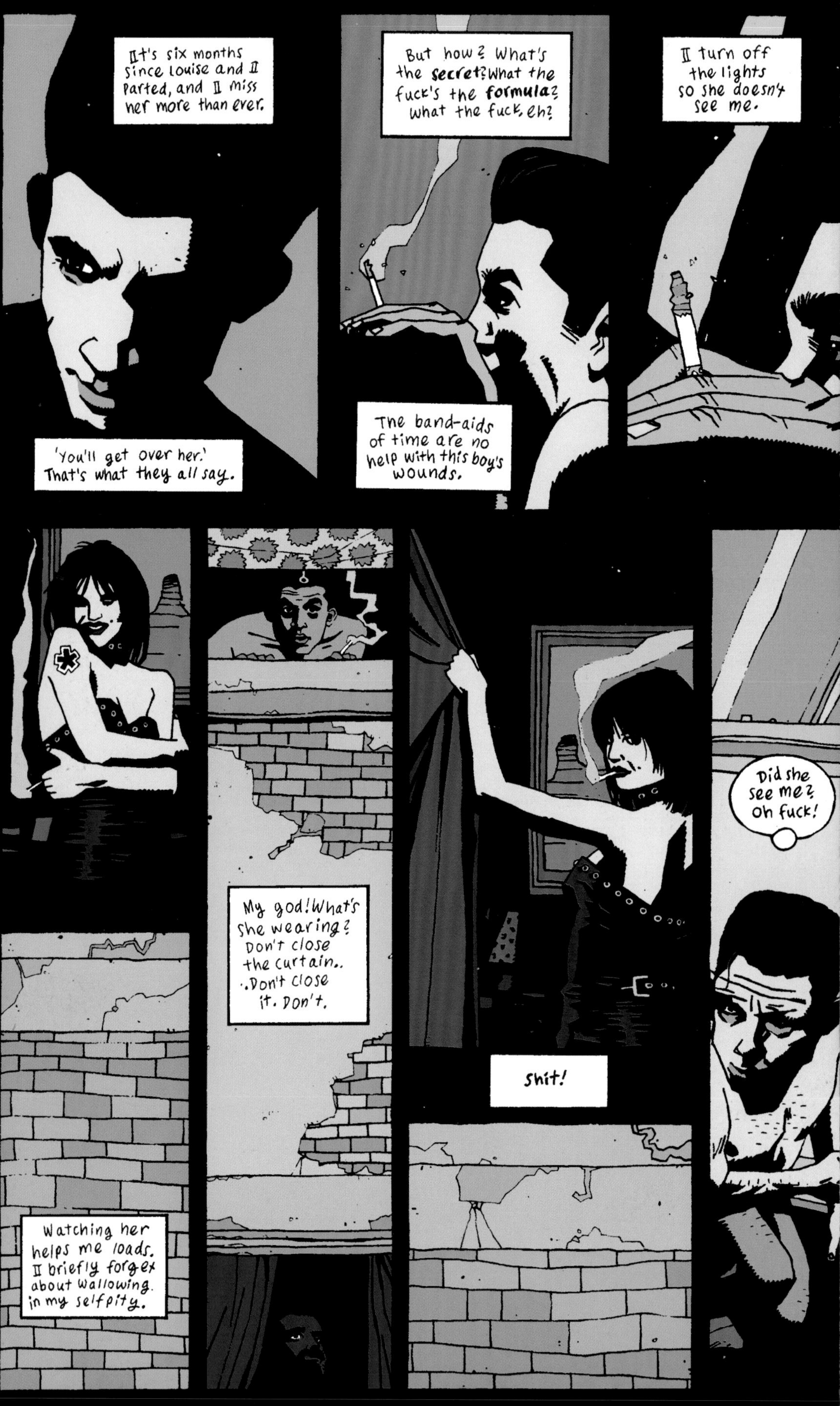
It's six months since Louise and I parted, and I miss her more than ever.
'You'll get over her.' That's what they all say.
But how? What's the secret? What the fuck's the formula? What the fuck, eh?
The band-aids of time are no help with this boy's wounds.
I turn off the lights so she doesn't see me.
Watching her helps me loads. I briefly forget about wallowing in my selfpity.
My god! What's she wearing? Don't close the curtain.. ..Don't close it. Don't.
Shit!
Did she see me? Oh fuck!

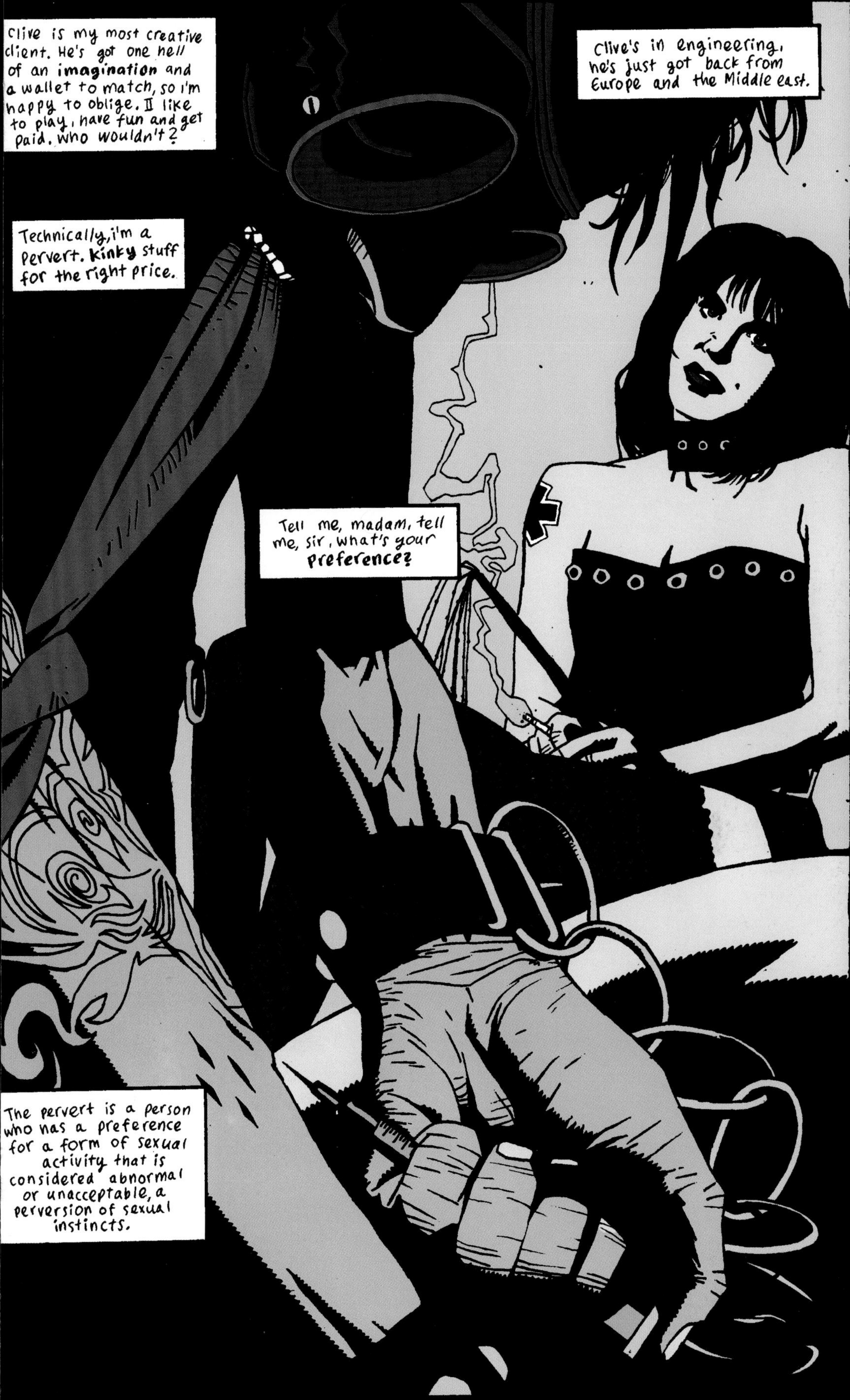
Clive is my most creative client. He's got one hell of an imagination and a wallet to match, so I'm happy to oblige. I like to play, have fun and get paid. who wouldn't?
Clive's in engineering, he's just got back from Europe and the Middle east.
Technically, i'm a pervert. kinky stuff for the right price.
Tell me, madam, tell me, sir, what's your preference?
The pervert is a person who has a preference for a form of sexual activity that is considered abnormal or unacceptable, a perversion of sexual instincts.

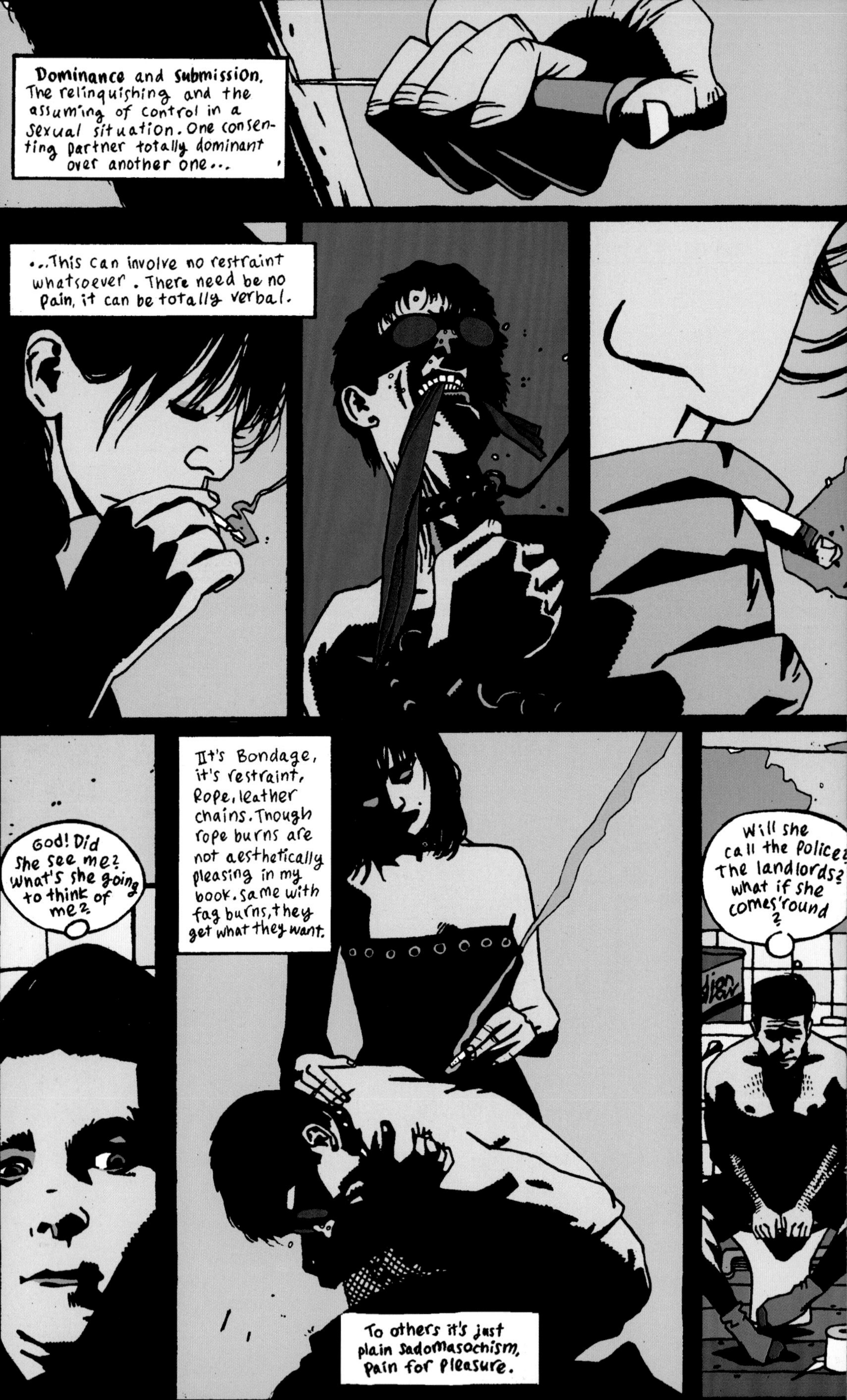
Dominance and Submission. The relinquishing and the assuming of control in a sexual situation. One consenting partner totally dominant over another one...
...This can involve no restraint whatsoever. There need be no pain, it can be totally verbal.
God! Did she see me? What's she going to think of me?
It's Bondage, it's restraint, rope, leather chains. Though rope burns are not aesthetically pleasing in my book. Same with fag burns, they get what they want.
Will she call the police? The landlords? What if she comes 'round?
To others it's just plain sadomasochism, pain for pleasure.

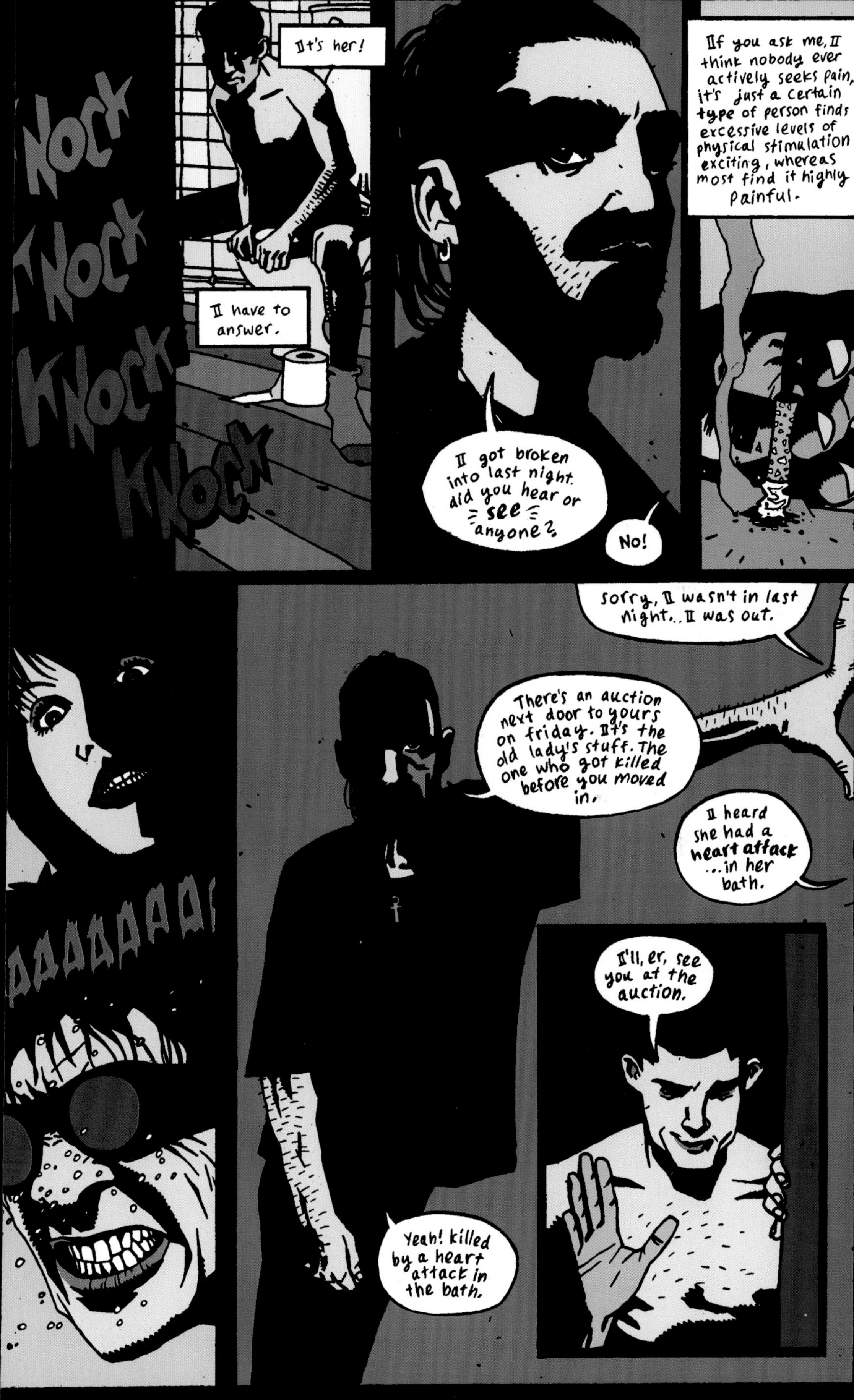

KNOCK KNOCK KNOCK KNOCK
It's her!
I have to answer.
I got broken into last night. did you hear or see anyone?
No!
If you ask me, I think nobody ever actively seeks pain, it's just a certain type of person finds excessive levels of physical stimulation exciting, whereas most find it highly painful.
AAAAAAAA
sorry, I wasn't in last night.. I was out.
There's an auction next door to yours on friday. It's the old lady's stuff. The one who got killed before you moved in.
I heard she had a heart attack ...in her bath.
Yeah! killed by a heart attack in the bath.
I'll, er, see you at the auction.

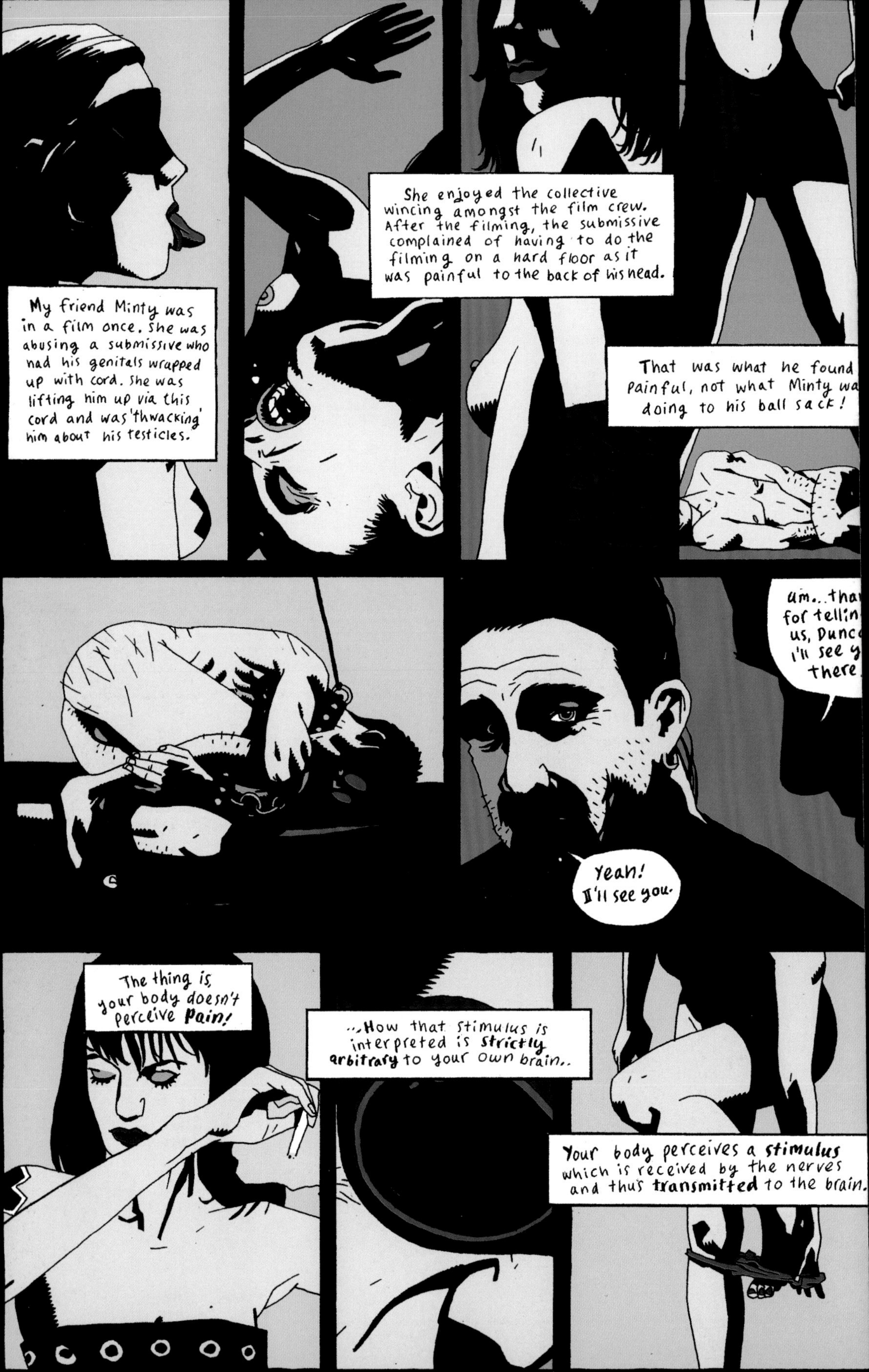
My friend Minty was in a film once. She was abusing a submissive who had his genitals wrapped up with cord. She was lifting him up via this cord and was 'thwacking' him about his testicles.
She enjoyed the collective wincing amongst the film crew. After the filming, the submissive complained of having to do the filming on a hard floor as it was painful to the back of his head.
That was what he found painful, not what Minty wa doing to his ball sack!
um... tha for tellin us, Dunc I'll see y there.
Yeah! I'll see you.
The thing is, your body doesn't perceive pain!
...How that stimulus is interpreted is strictly arbitrary to your own brain..
Your body perceives a stimulus which is received by the nerves and thus transmitted to the brain.

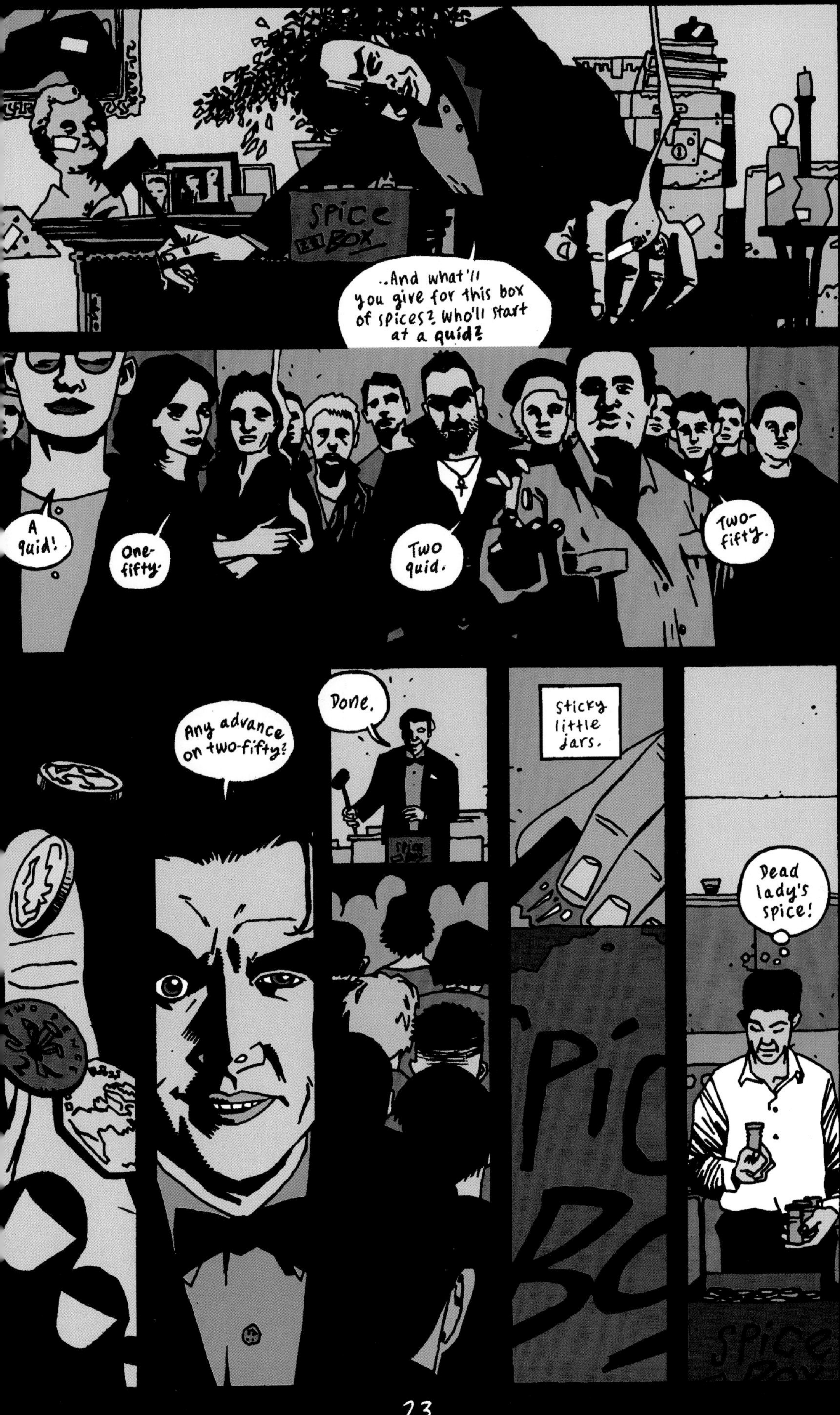
..And what'll you give for this box of spices? Who'll start at a quid?
A quid!
One-fifty.
Two quid.
Two-fifty.
Any advance on two-fifty?
Done.
Sticky little jars.
Dead lady's spice!

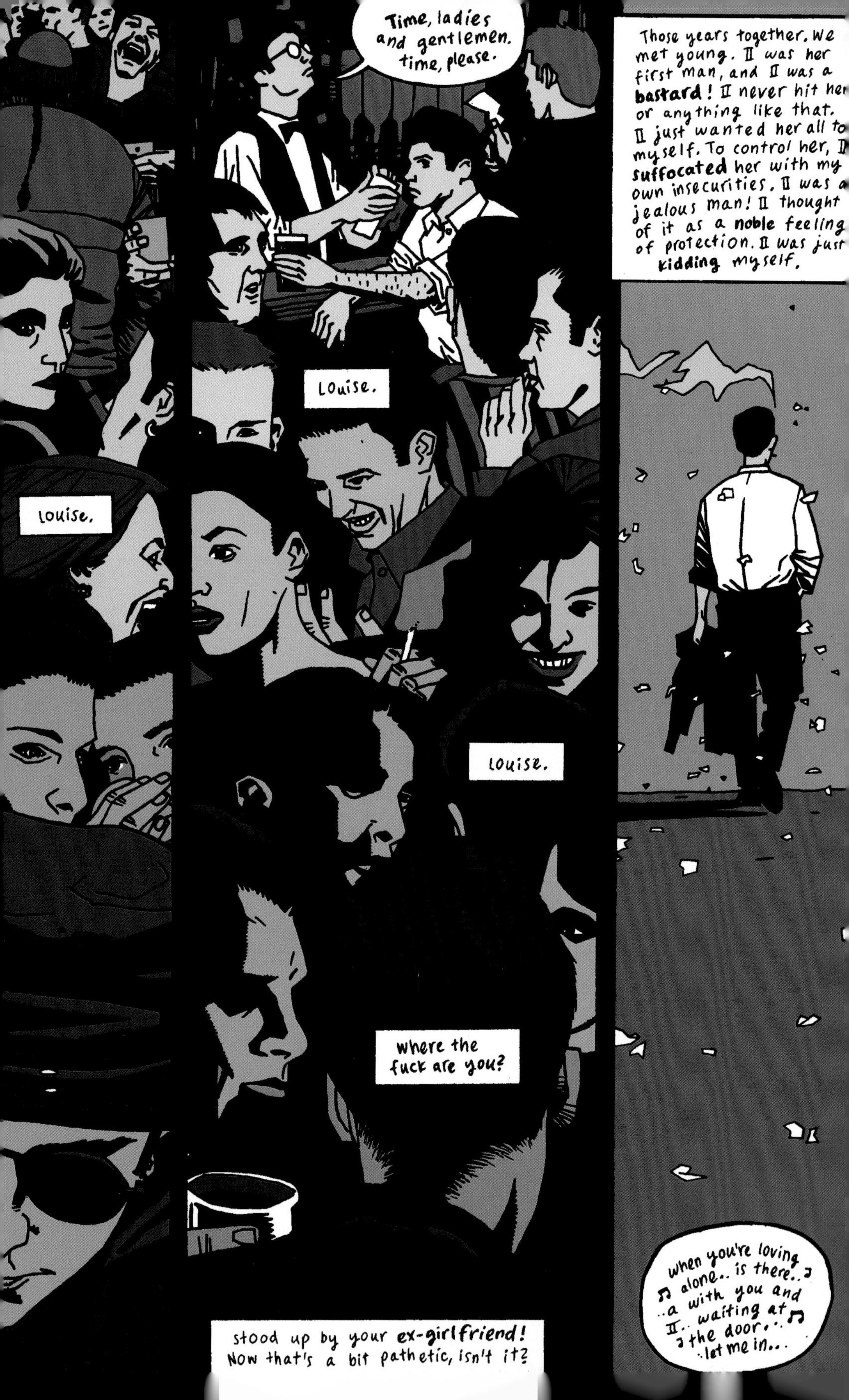
Time, ladies and gentlemen. time, please.
Those years together. We met young. I was her first man, and I was a **bastard**! I never hit her or anything like that. I just wanted her all to myself. To control her, I **suffocated** her with my own insecurities. I was a jealous man! I thought of it as a **noble** feeling of protection. I was just **kidding** myself.
Louise.
louise.
louise.
where the fuck are you?
stood up by your **ex-girlfriend**! Now that's a bit pathetic, isn't it?
when you're loving alone.. is there.. a with you and I.. waiting at the door... let me in...

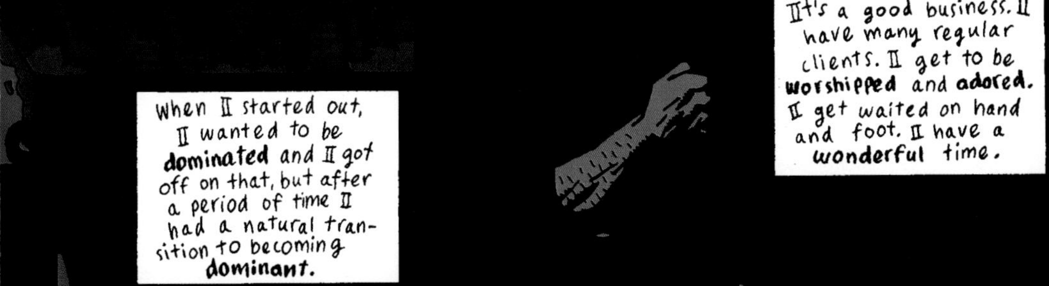
When I started out, I wanted to be **dominated** and I got off on that, but after a period of time I had a natural transition to becoming **dominant.**
It's a good business. I have many regular clients. I get to be **worshipped** and **adored.** I get waited on hand and foot. I have a **wonderful** time.

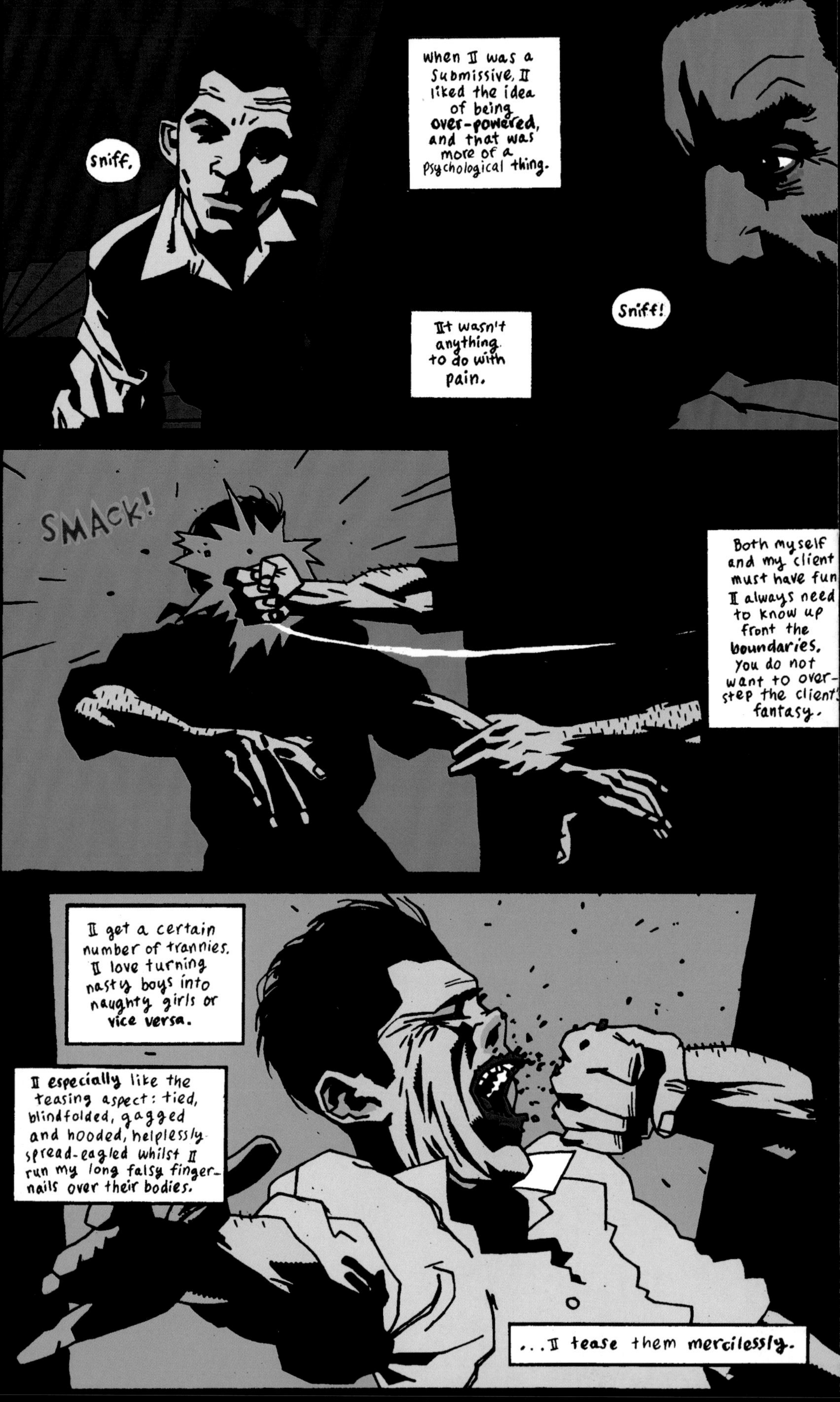

When I was a submissive, I liked the idea of being over-powered, and that was more of a psychological thing.
Sniff.
It wasn't anything to do with pain.
Sniff!
SMACK!
Both myself and my client must have fun I always need to know up front the boundaries. You do not want to over-step the client's fantasy.
I get a certain number of trannies. I love turning nasty boys into naughty girls or vice versa.
I especially like the teasing aspect: tied, blindfolded, gagged and hooded, helplessly spread-eagled whilst I run my long falsy finger-nails over their bodies.
...I tease them mercilessly.

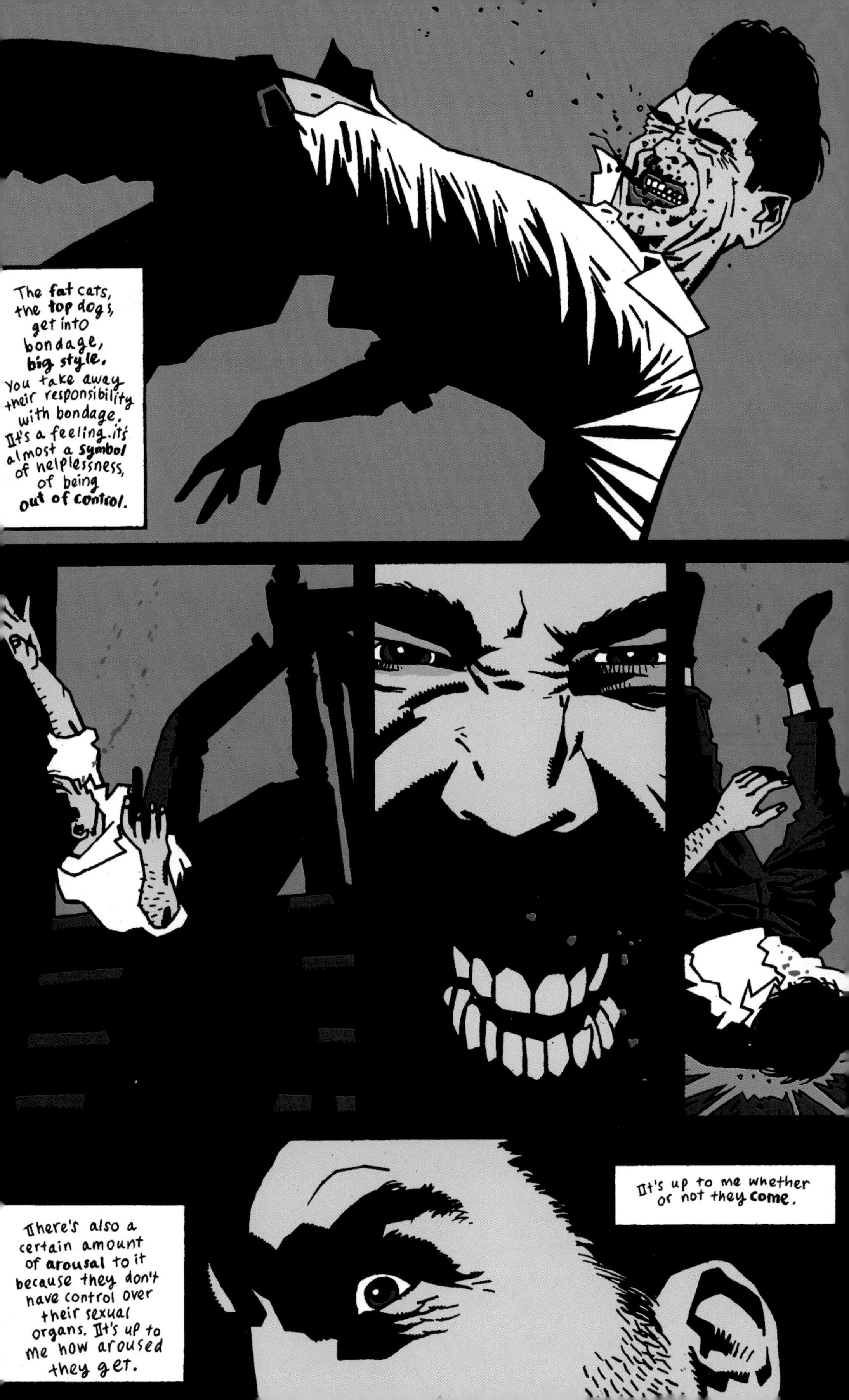
The fat cats, the top dogs, get into bondage, big style. You take away their responsibility with bondage. It's a feeling. it's almost a symbol of helplessness, of being out of control.
There's also a certain amount of arousal to it because they don't have control over their sexual organs. It's up to me how aroused they get.
It's up to me whether or not they come.

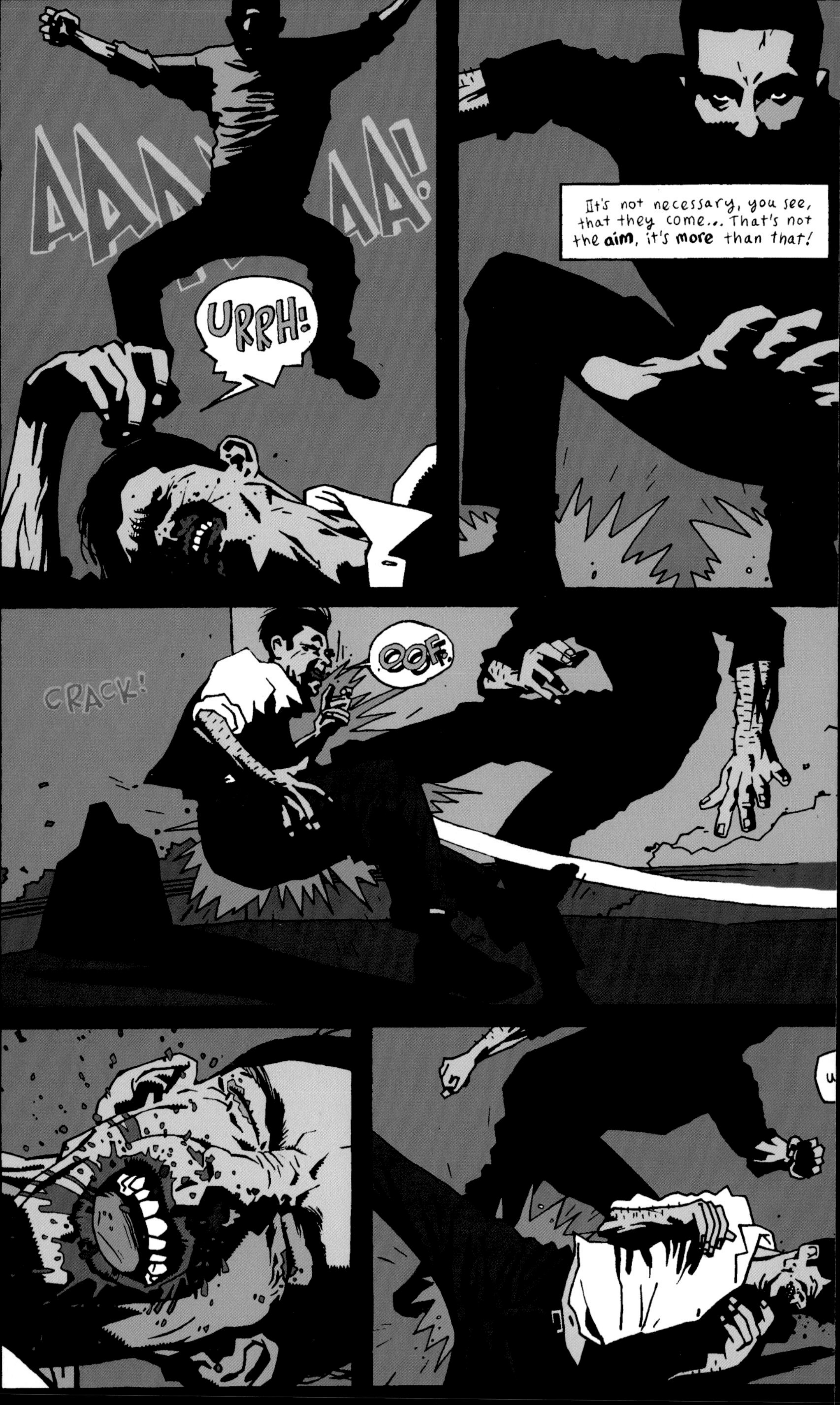
AAAA AA!
URRH!
It's not necessary, you see, that they come... That's not the **aim**, it's **more** than that!
CRACK!
OOF.

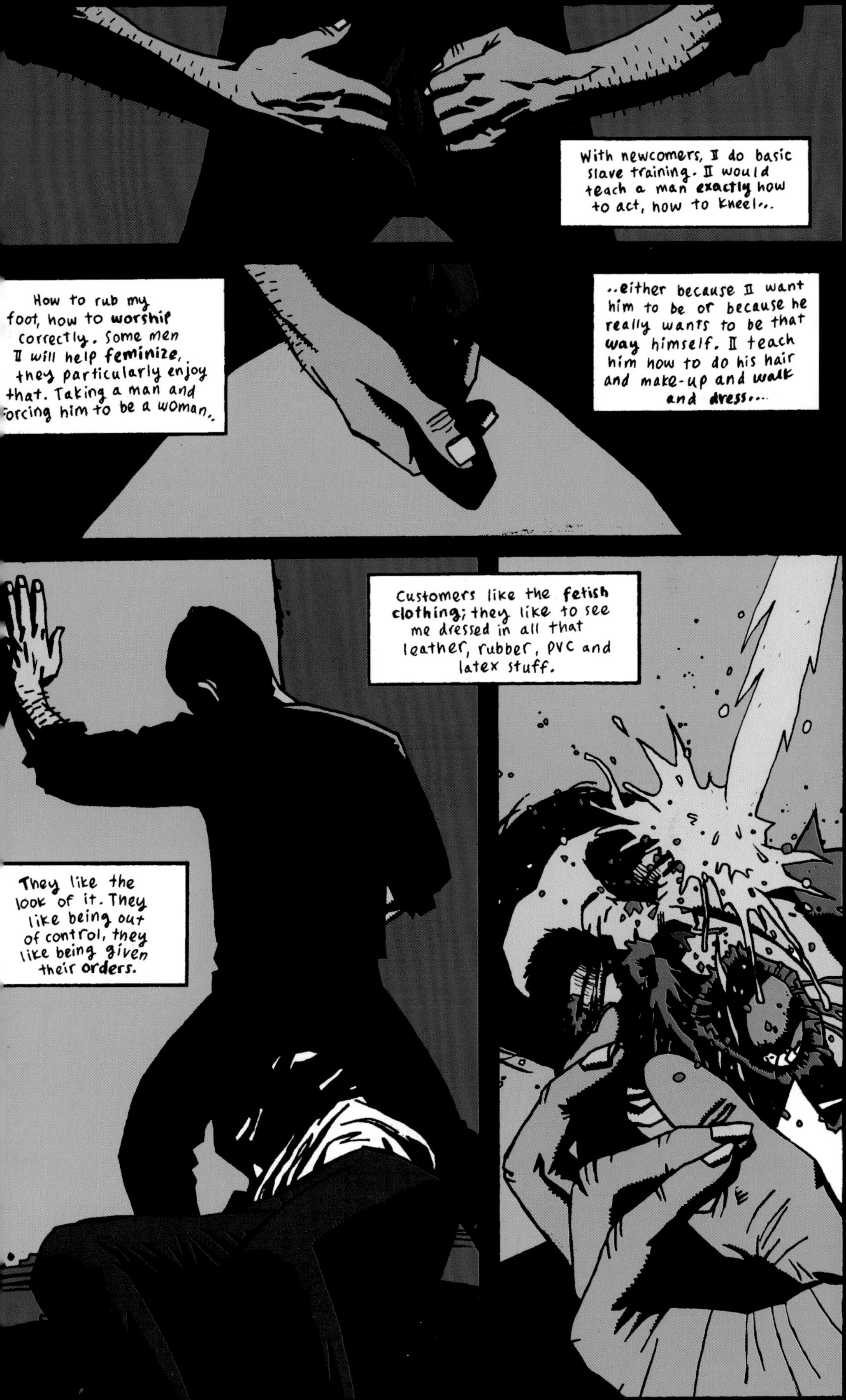
With newcomers, I do basic slave training. I would teach a man exactly how to act, how to kneel...
How to rub my foot, how to worship correctly. Some men I will help feminize, they particularly enjoy that. Taking a man and forcing him to be a woman..
..either because I want him to be or because he really wants to be that way himself. I teach him how to do his hair and make-up and walk and dress...
Customers like the fetish clothing; they like to see me dressed in all that leather, rubber, PVC and latex stuff.
They like the look of it. They like being out of control, they like being given their orders.

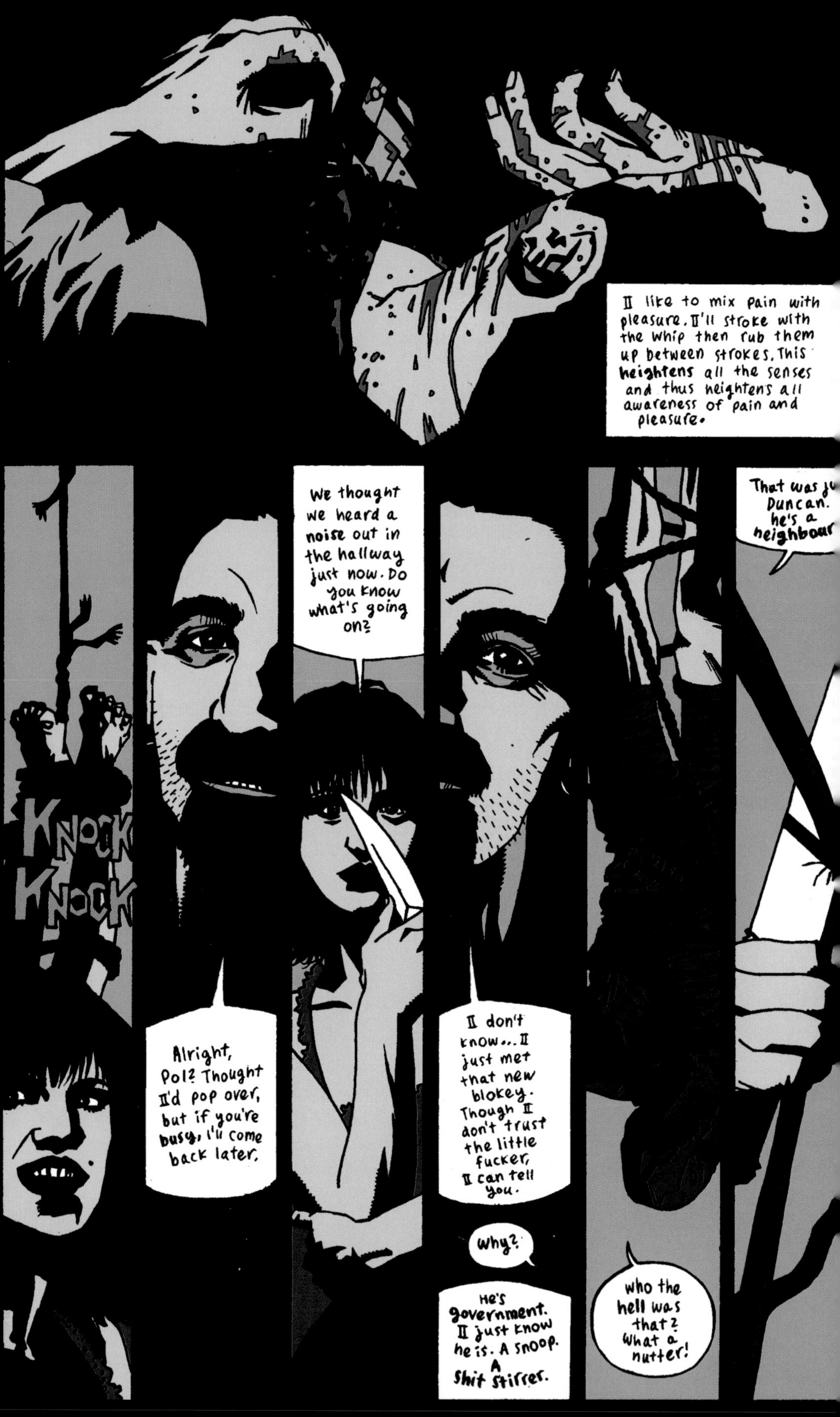
I like to mix pain with pleasure. I'll stroke with the whip then rub them up between strokes. This heightens all the senses and thus heightens all awareness of pain and pleasure.
KNOCK KNOCK
We thought we heard a noise out in the hallway just now. Do you know what's going on?
That was ju
Duncan. He's a neighbour
Alright, Pol? Thought I'd pop over, but if you're busy, I'll come back later.
I don't know... I just met that new blokey. Though I don't trust the little fucker, I can tell you.
Why?
He's government. I just know he is. A snoop. A shit stirrer.
Who the hell was that? What a nutter!

I'm seventy and I'm out of here soon, now my friend is gone. I'll miss Mrs. Hitchens, I will.

Blind as a bat, me, but my **sonar** is good, oh yes. And I sense something. I heard it, now I can smell it.

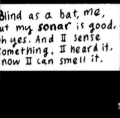

Damp permeates this place. Does me no good. But that's something else. sniff.. sniff...

..sniff.. sniff... piss! drinker's piss. I know that smell. Heightened awareness, me, smelt it a mile off. Am I... right or am I wrong?

?

Who's that?

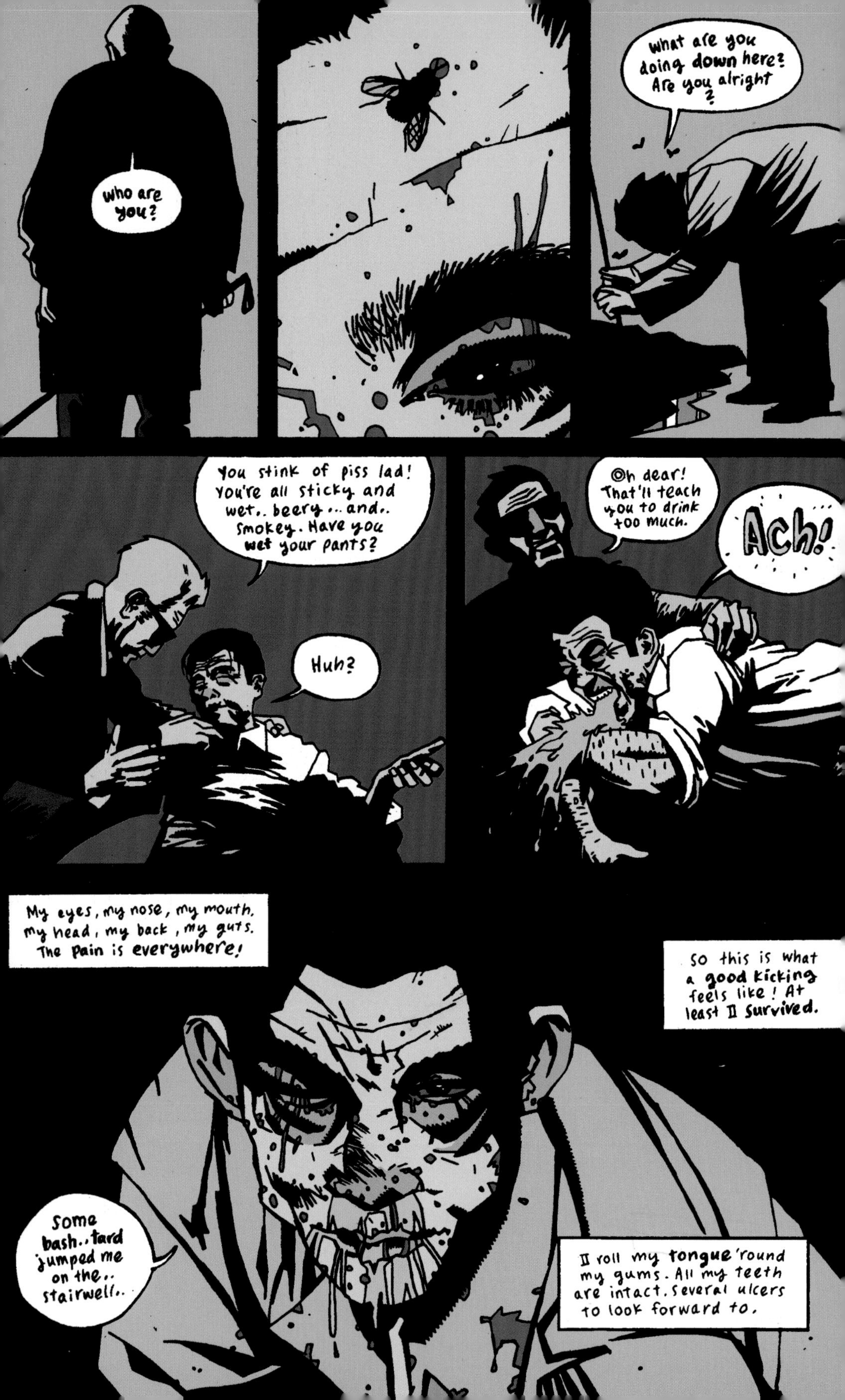

who are you?
What are you doing down here? Are you alright?
You stink of piss lad! You're all sticky and wet.. beery... and.. smokey. Have you wet your pants?
Huh?
Oh dear! That'll teach you to drink too much.
Ach!
My eyes, my nose, my mouth, my head, my back, my guts. The pain is everywhere!
So this is what a good kicking feels like! At least I survived.
Some bash.. tard jumped me on the.. stairwell..
I roll my tongue 'round my gums. All my teeth are intact. Several ulcers to look forward to.

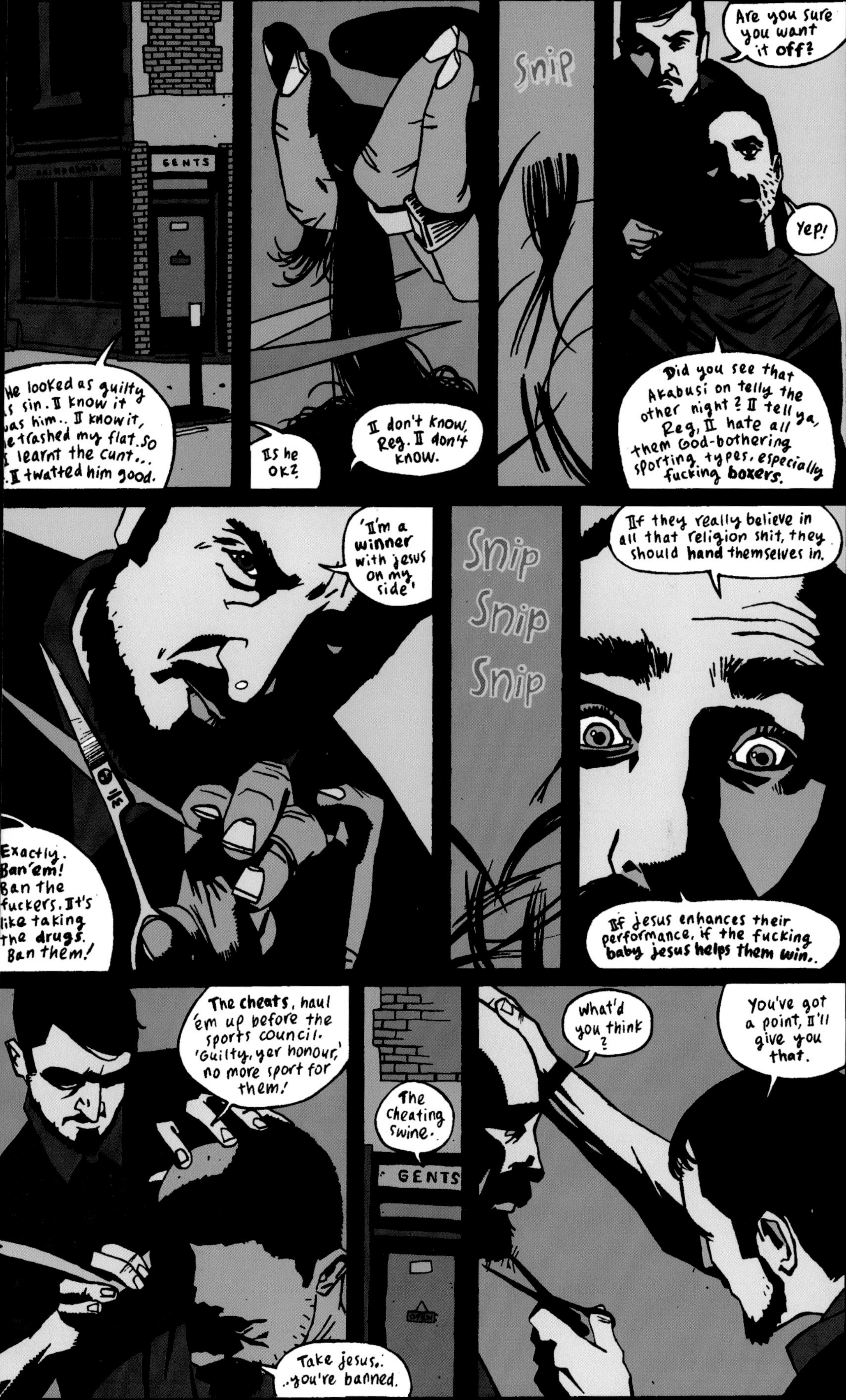

He looked as guilty as sin. I know it was him.. I know it, he trashed my flat. So I learnt the cunt... ..I twatted him good.
Is he OK?
I don't know, Reg. I don't know.
Snip
Are you sure you want it off?
Yep!
Did you see that Akabusi on telly the other night? I tell ya, Reg, I hate all them God-bothering sporting types, especially fucking boxers.
'I'm a winner with jesus on my side'
Exactly. Ban 'em! Ban the fuckers. It's like taking the drugs. Ban them!
Snip Snip Snip
If they really believe in all that religion shit, they should hand themselves in.
If jesus enhances their performance, if the fucking baby jesus helps them win..
The cheats, haul 'em up before the sports council. 'Guilty, yer honour,' no more sport for them!
Take jesus.. ..you're banned.
The cheating swine.
GENTS
What'd you think?
You've got a point, I'll give you that.

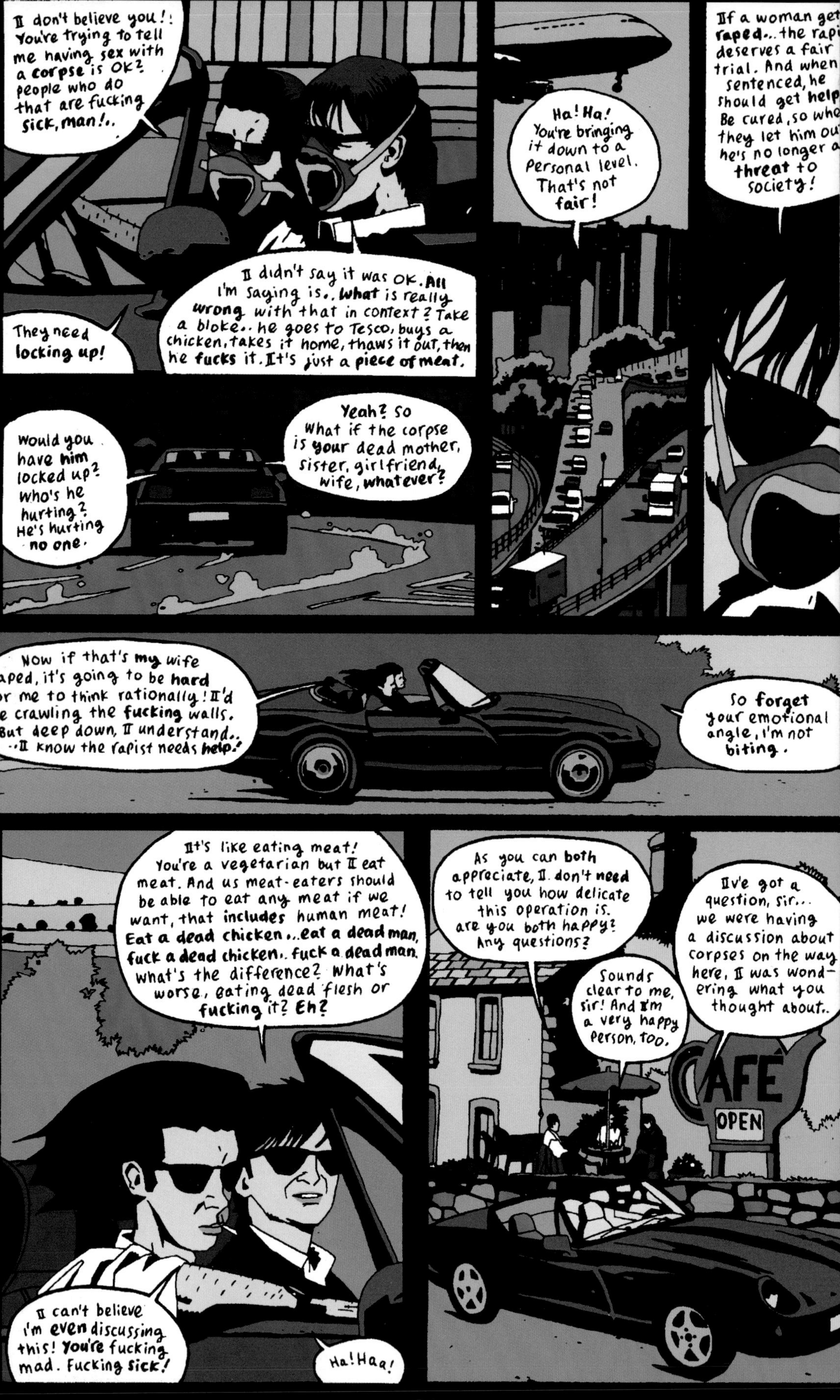

I don't believe you!: You're trying to tell me having sex with a corpse is OK? people who do that are fucking sick, man!..
They need locking up!
I didn't say it was OK. All I'm saying is.. what is really wrong with that in context? Take a bloke.. he goes to Tesco, buys a chicken, takes it home, thaws it out, then he fucks it. It's just a piece of meat.
Ha! Ha! You're bringing it down to a personal level. That's not fair!
If a woman get raped.. the rapi deserves a fair trial. And when sentenced, he should get help Be cured, so whe they let him ou he's no longer a threat to society!
Would you have him locked up? who's he hurting? He's hurting no one.
Yeah? So what if the corpse is your dead mother, sister, girlfriend, wife, whatever?
Now if that's my wife raped, it's going to be hard for me to think rationally! I'd be crawling the fucking walls. But deep down, I understand.. ..I know the rapist needs help!
So forget your emotional angle, I'm not biting.
It's like eating meat! You're a vegetarian but I eat meat. And us meat-eaters should be able to eat any meat if we want, that includes human meat! Eat a dead chicken...eat a dead man, fuck a dead chicken.. fuck a dead man. What's the difference? What's worse, eating dead flesh or fucking it? Eh?
I can't believe I'm even discussing this! You're fucking mad. Fucking sick!
Ha! Haa!
As you can both appreciate, I don't need to tell you how delicate this operation is. are you both happy? Any questions?
Sounds clear to me, sir! And I'm a very happy person, too.
I've got a question, sir... we were having a discussion about corpses on the way here, I was wondering what you thought about..
CAFÉ
OPEN

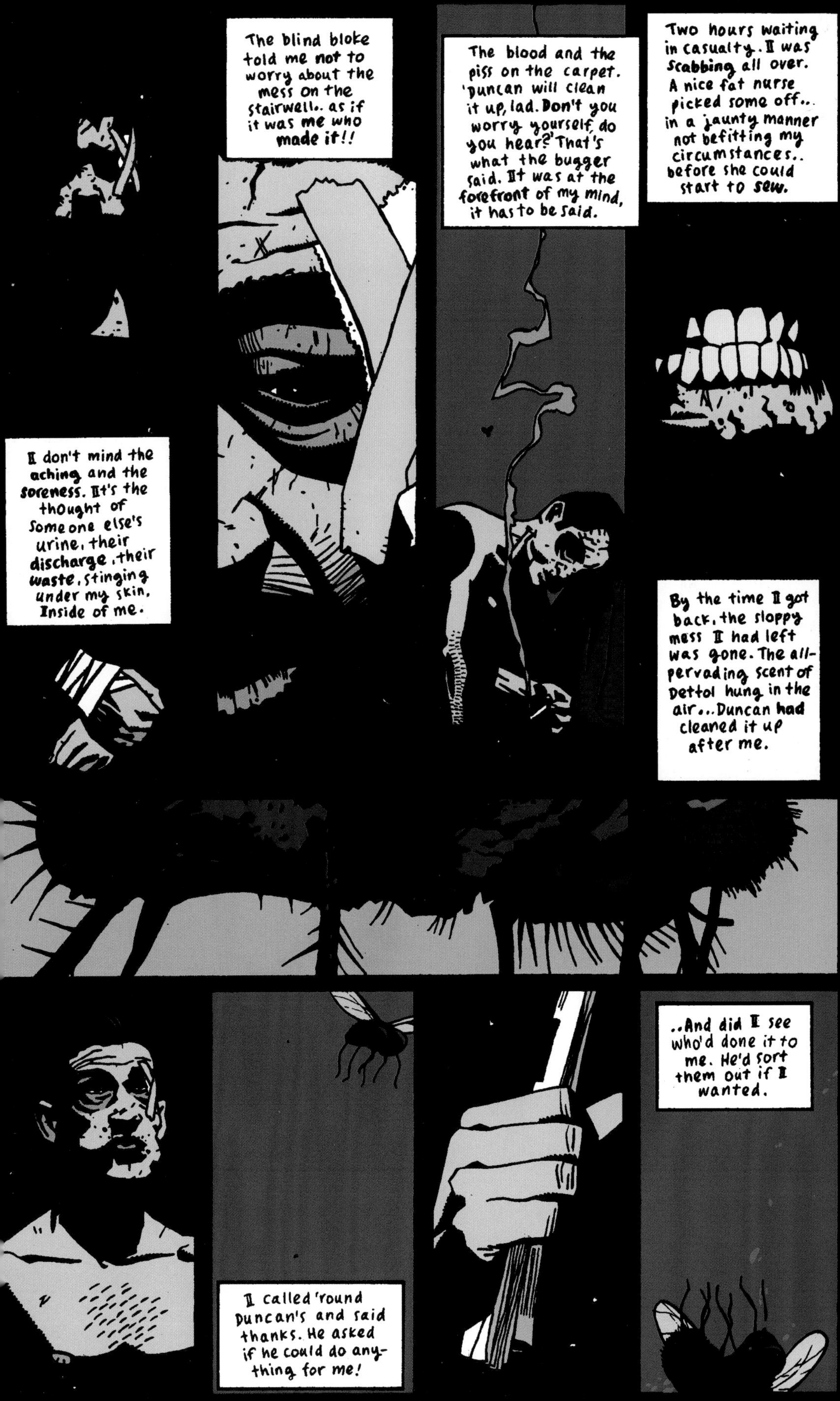
The blind bloke told me not to worry about the mess on the stairwell.. as if it was me who made it!!
The blood and the piss on the carpet. 'Duncan will clean it up, lad. Don't you worry yourself, do you hear?' That's what the bugger said. It was at the forefront of my mind, it has to be said.
Two hours waiting in casualty. I was scabbing all over. A nice fat nurse picked some off.. in a jaunty manner not befitting my circumstances.. before she could start to sew.
I don't mind the aching and the soreness. It's the thought of Someone else's urine, their discharge, their waste, stinging under my skin. Inside of me.
By the time I got back, the sloppy mess I had left was gone. The all-pervading scent of Dettol hung in the air...Duncan had cleaned it up after me.
I called 'round Duncan's and said thanks. He asked if he could do anything for me!
..And did I see who'd done it to me. He'd sort them out if I wanted.

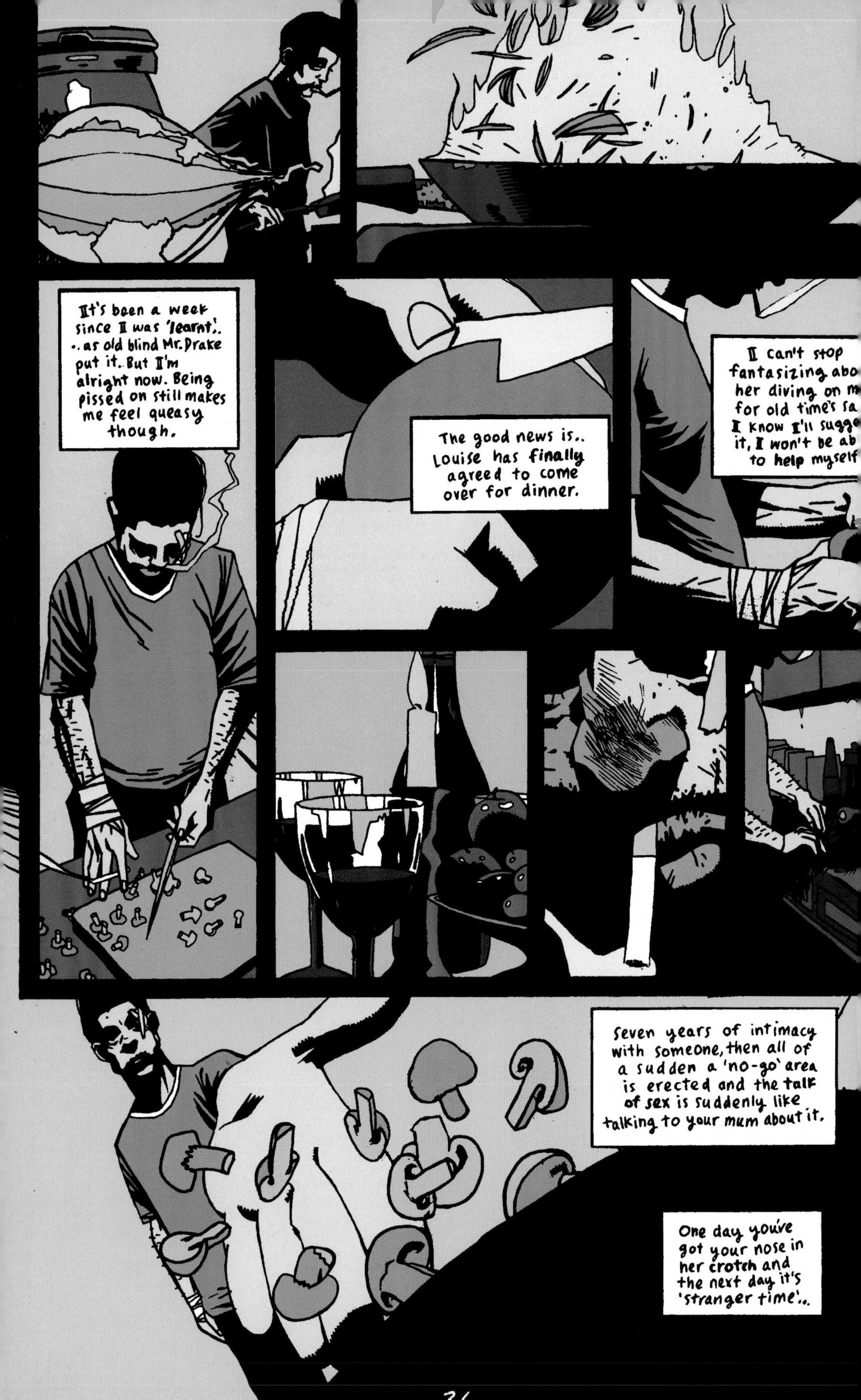
It's been a week since I was 'learnt'.. ..as old blind Mr. Drake put it.. But I'm alright now. Being pissed on still makes me feel queasy though.
The good news is.. Louise has finally agreed to come over for dinner.
I can't stop fantasizing abo her diving on m for old time's sa I know I'll sugge it, I won't be ab to help myself
Seven years of intimacy with someone, then all of a sudden a 'no-go' area is erected and the talk of sex is suddenly like talking to your mum about it.
One day you've got your nose in her crotch and the next day it's 'stranger time'..

Duncan knocks to borrow milk for the umpteenth time. I think he just came around to show off his new head! Sometimes I think the milk's just an excuse to chat to me. Why he needs an excuse is beyond me. I just wish he wouldn't drink my bloody milk all the time.

D'ya like it, charlie-boy? Eh? D'ya?

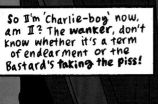

So I'm 'Charlie-boy' now, am I? The wanker, don't know whether it's a term of endearment or the Bastard's taking the piss!

Jesus Christ!

Wow! Does God exist?

There's a man who lives in that flat opposite. See that window? That's his. My friend Duncan says he's in tonight. He likes to watch me. He thinks I don't know. It's more fun that way.

The tosser!

Can he see us?

He's looking..

She's got a friend!!

Chicken choking "Charlie-boy"! Bless him..

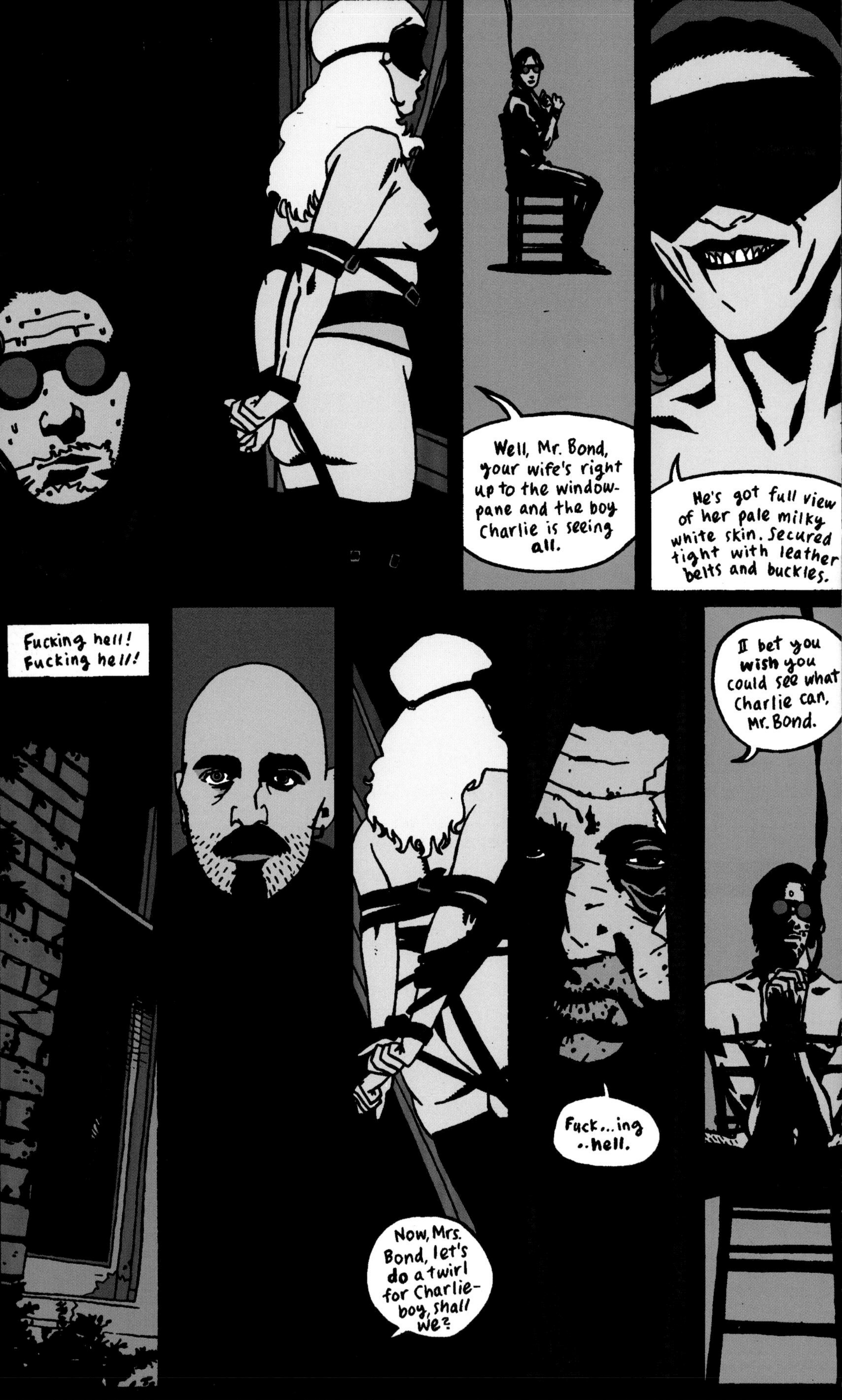
Well, Mr. Bond, your wife's right up to the window-pane and the boy Charlie is seeing all.
He's got full view of her pale milky white skin. Secured tight with leather belts and buckles.
Fucking hell! Fucking hell!
I bet you wish you could see what Charlie can, Mr. Bond.
Fuck...ing ..hell.
Now, Mrs. Bond, let's do a twirl for Charlie-boy, shall we?

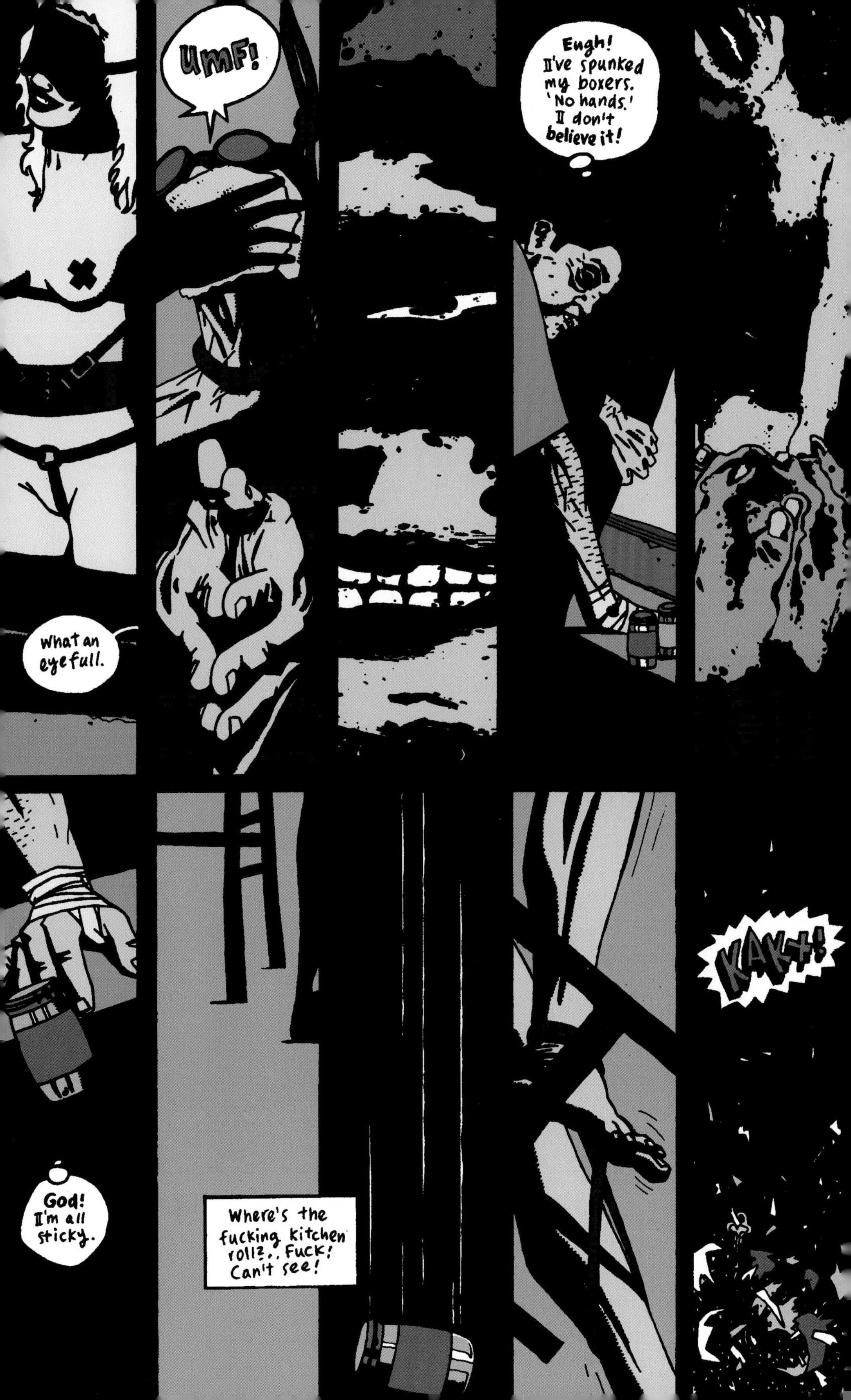
UMF!
Eugh! I've spunked my boxers. 'No hands.' I don't believe it!
What an eyefull.
God! I'm all sticky.
Where's the fucking kitchen roll?.. Fuck! Can't see!
KAKT!

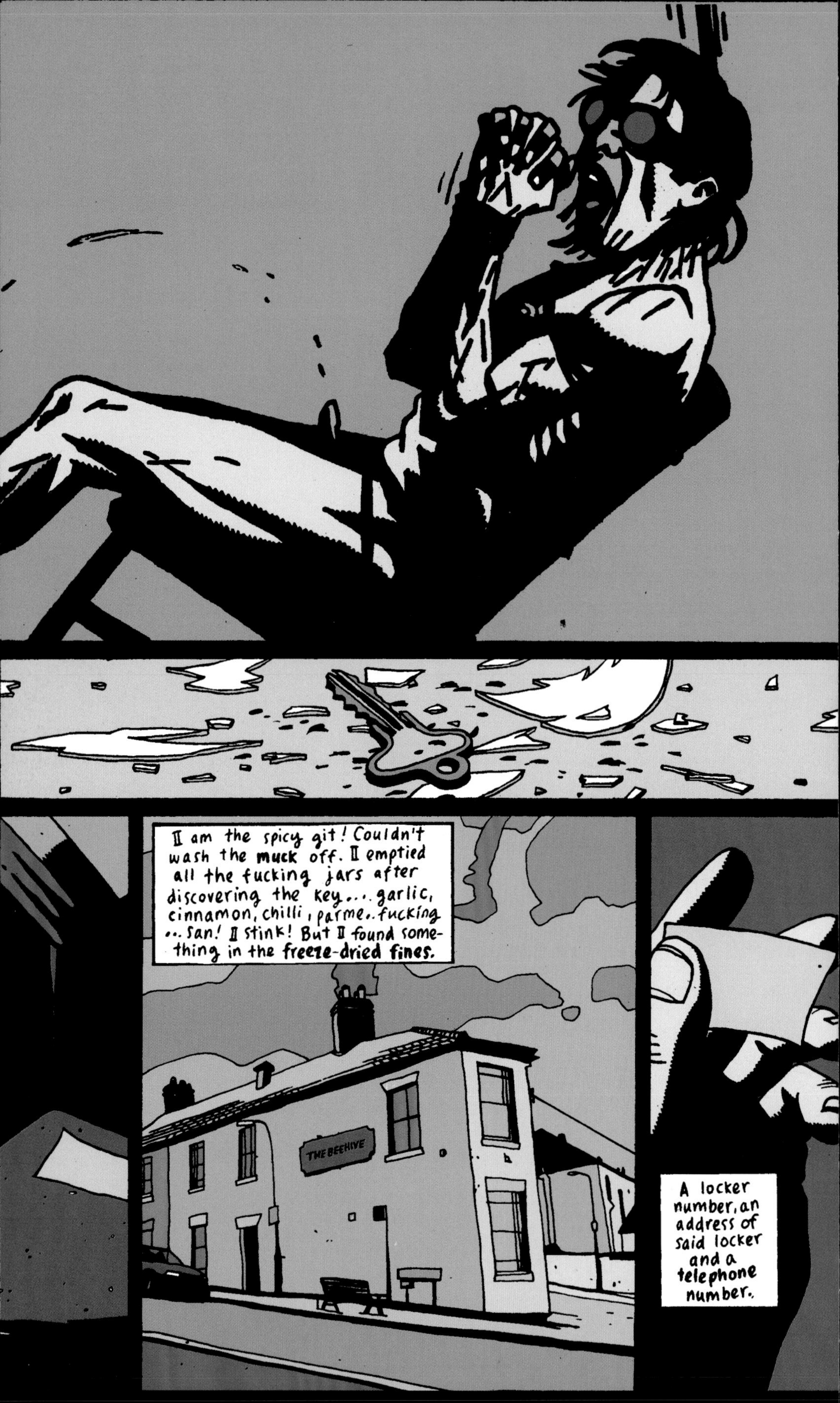
I am the spicy git! Couldn't wash the muck off. I emptied all the fucking jars after discovering the key.... garlic, cinnamon, chilli, parme.. fucking ...san! I stink! But I found something in the freeze-dried fines.
THE BEEHIVE
A locker number, an address of said locker and a telephone number.

See you again!

I just stepped out of my flat on the top stairs landing.

Were they... was she the ..?

..You're a professional after all.

You were briefed this morning. You read of her movements compiled by 'the team'. Thorough work. She's on time.. You think she's clocked you.. ..but no matter..

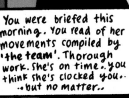

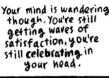

You rendered a Jehovah's witness speechless. It was a fine moment.

Your mind is wandering though. You're still getting waves of satisfaction. You're still celebrating in your head.

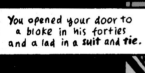

You opened your door to a bloke in his forties and a lad in a suit and tie.

The bloke wore an anorak.

After parrying the usual thrust of questions and having the obligatory **watchtower** shoved into your mitt.

..you hit back.

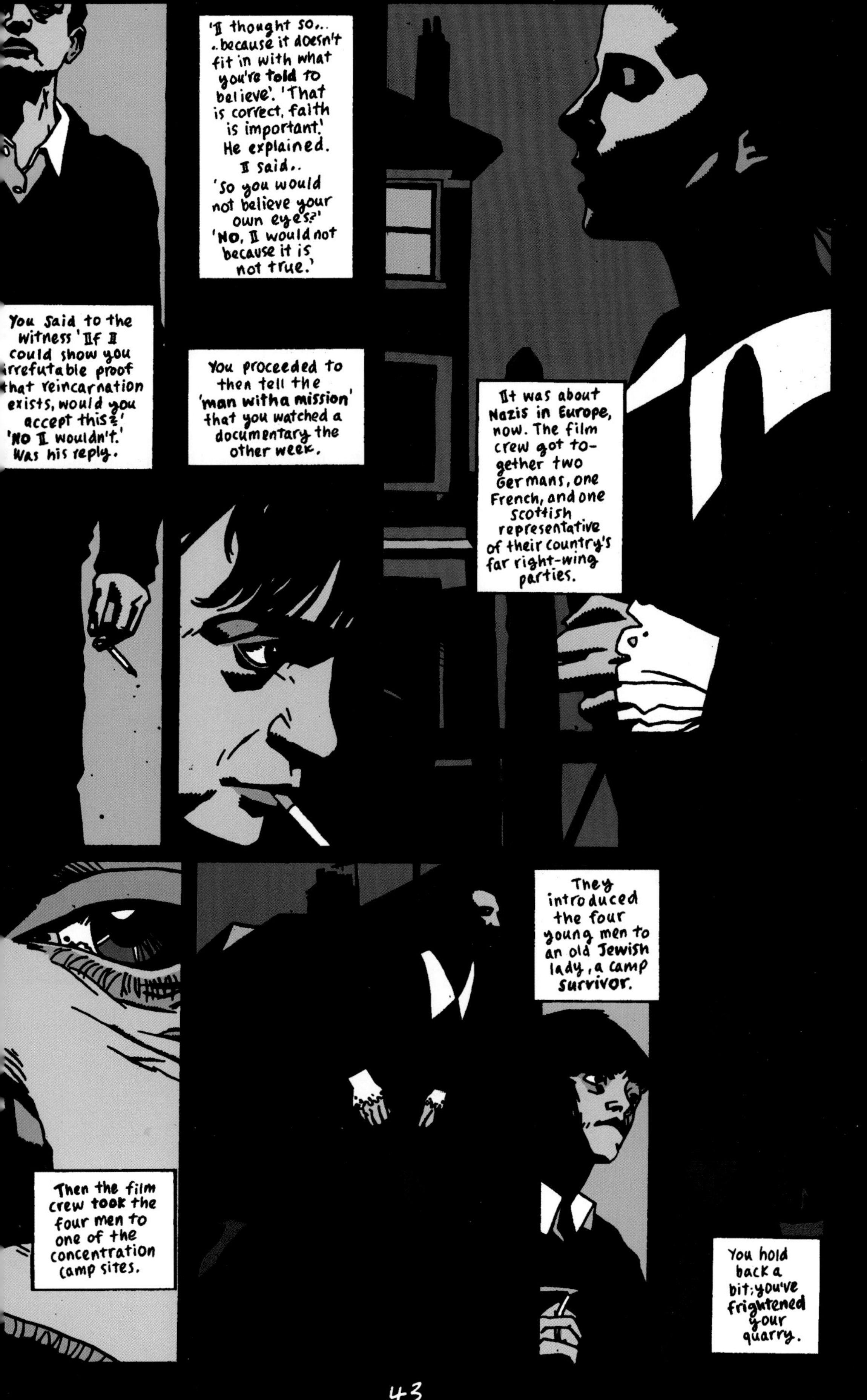
'I thought so... ..because it doesn't fit in with what you're told to believe'. 'That is correct, faith is important.' He explained. I said.. 'So you would not believe your own eyes?' 'NO, I would not because it is not true.'
You said to the witness 'If I could show you irrefutable proof that reincarnation exists, would you accept this?' 'NO I wouldn't.' Was his reply.
You proceeded to then tell the 'man with a mission' that you watched a documentary the other week.
It was about Nazis in Europe, now. The film crew got together two Germans, one French, and one Scottish representative of their country's far right-wing parties.
They introduced the four young men to an old Jewish lady, a camp survivor.
Then the film crew took the four men to one of the concentration camp sites.
You hold back a bit; you've frightened your quarry.

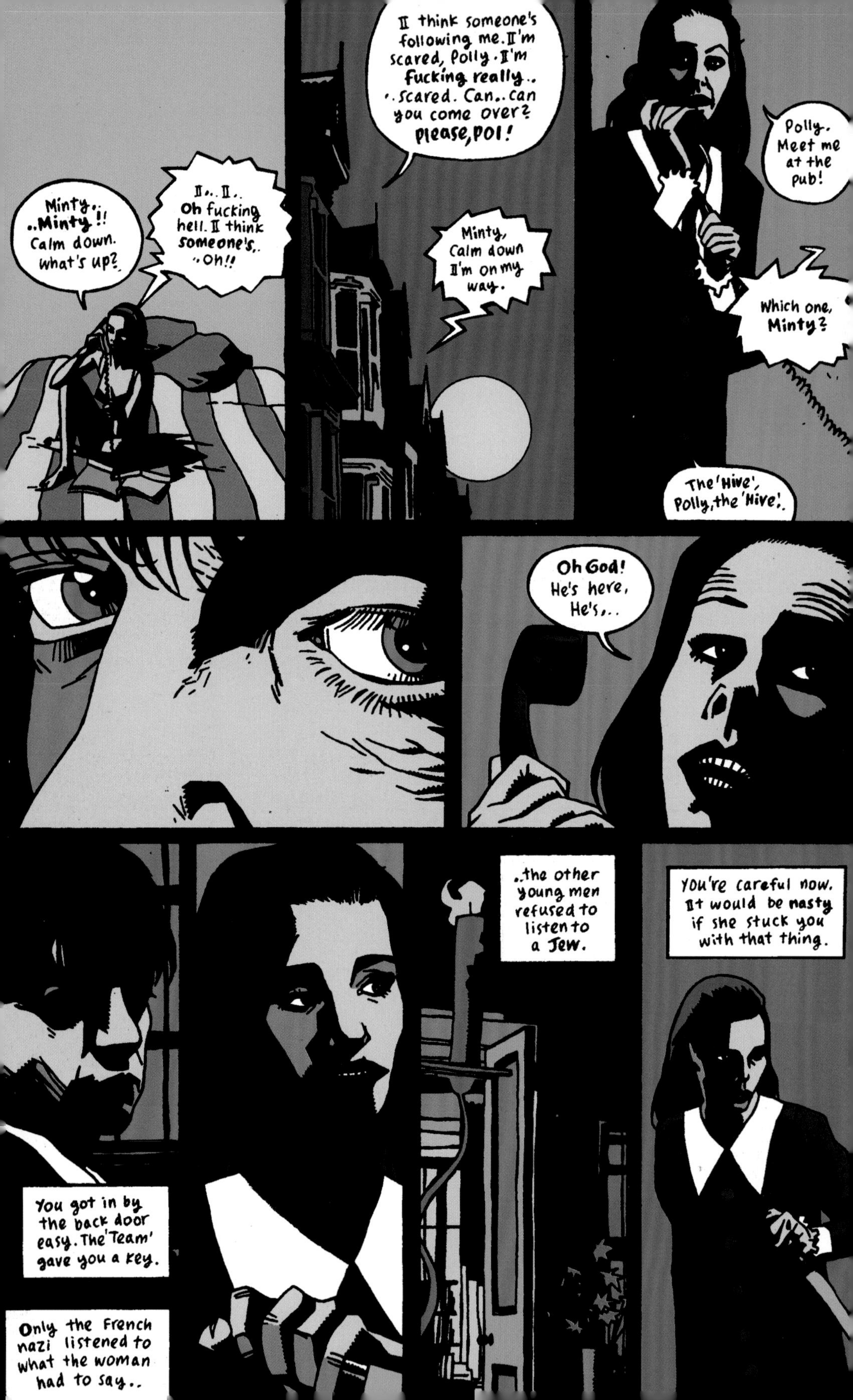
Minty.. ..Minty!! Calm down. What's up?
I.. I.. Oh fucking hell. I think someone's.. ..Oh!!
I think someone's following me. I'm scared, Polly. I'm fucking really.. ..scared. Can..can you come over? Please, Pol!
Minty, Calm down I'm on my way.
Polly. Meet me at the pub!
Which one, Minty?
The 'Hive', Polly, the 'Hive'.
Oh God! He's here, He's..
You got in by the back door easy. The 'Team' gave you a key.
Only the French nazi listened to what the woman had to say..
..the other young men refused to listen to a Jew.
You're careful now. It would be nasty if she stuck you with that thing.

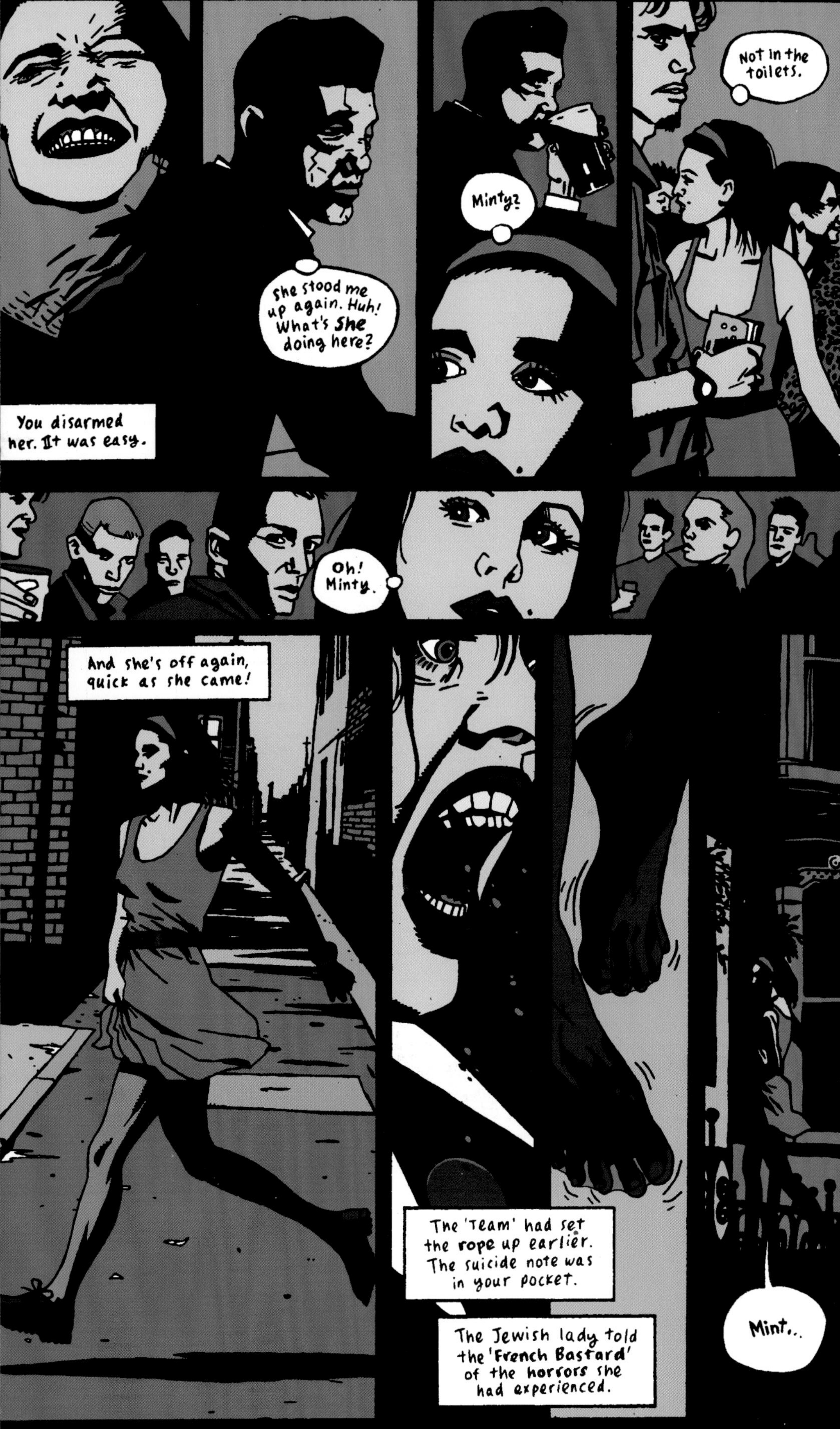
You disarmed her. It was easy.
She stood me up again. Huh! What's She doing here?
Minty?
Not in the toilets.
Oh! Minty.
And she's off again, quick as she came!
The 'Team' had set the rope up earlier. The suicide note was in your pocket.
The Jewish lady told the 'French Bastard' of the horrors she had experienced.
Mint..

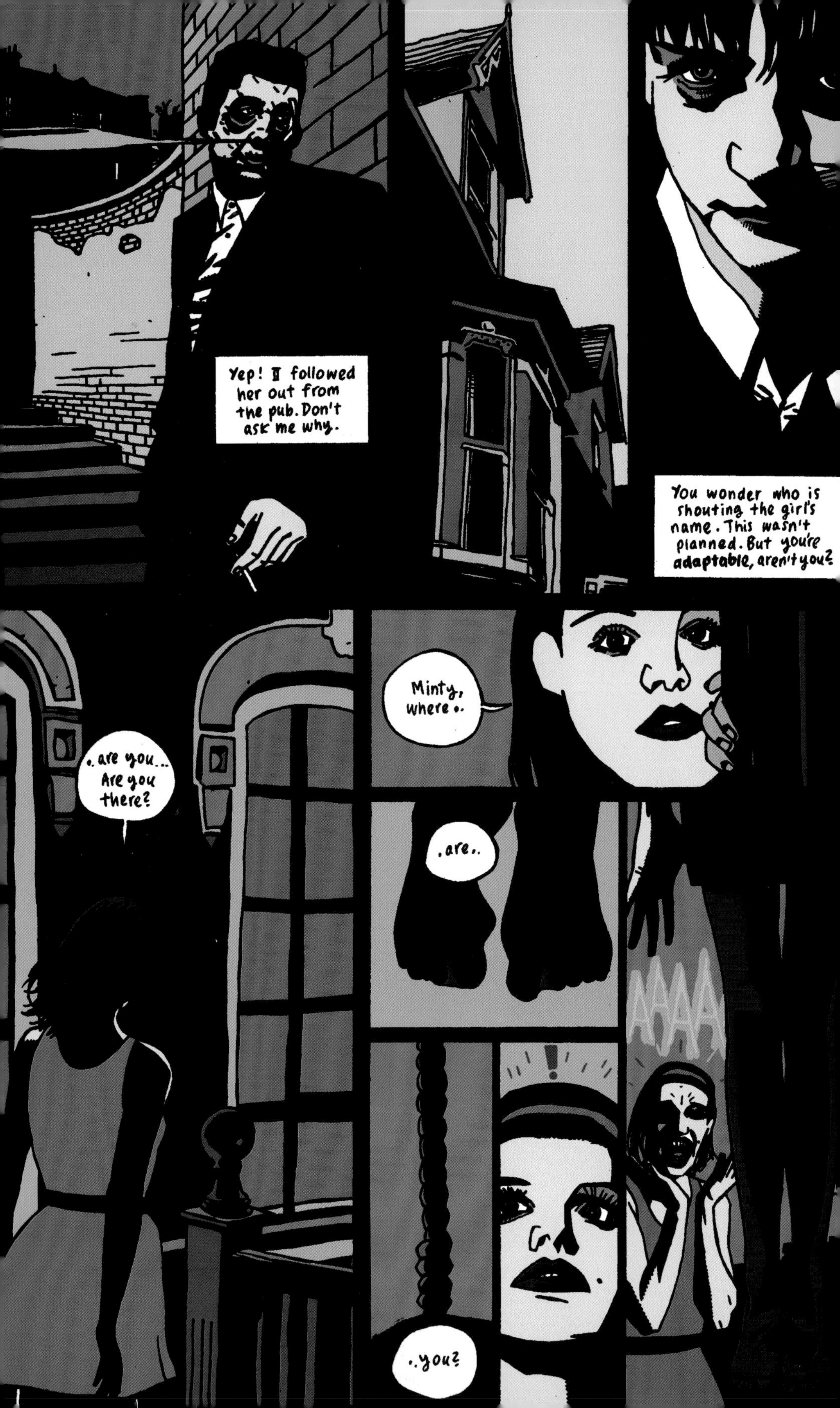
Yep! I followed her out from the pub. Don't ask me why.
You wonder who is shouting the girl's name. This wasn't planned. But you're adaptable, aren't you?
..are you... Are you there?
Minty, where..
.are..
AAAA
..you?

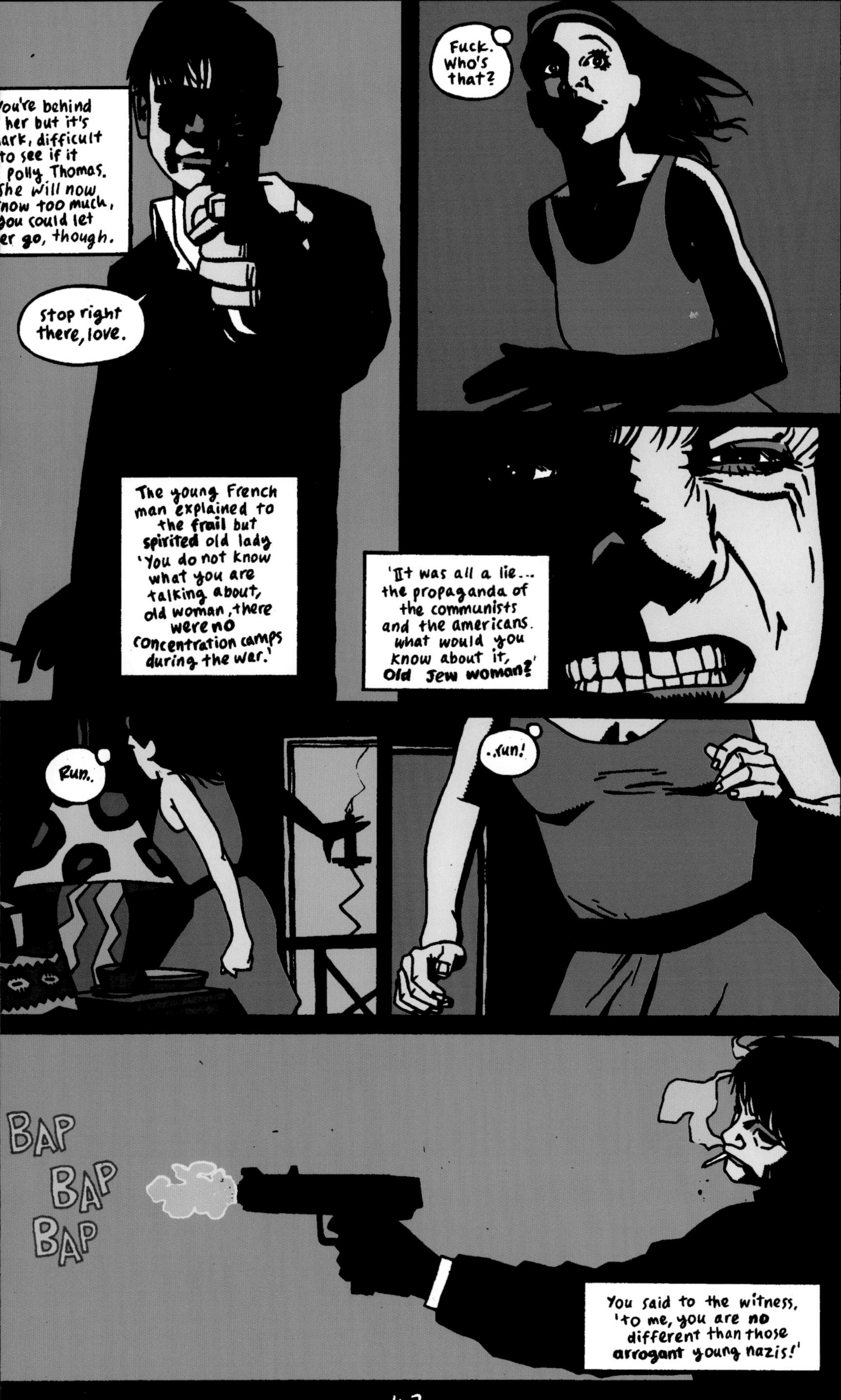

You're behind her but it's dark, difficult to see if it Polly Thomas. She will now know too much, you could let her go, though.
Stop right there, love.
Fuck. Who's that?
The young French man explained to the frail but spirited old lady 'You do not know what you are talking about, old woman, there were no concentration camps during the war.'
'It was all a lie... the propaganda of the communists and the americans. What would you know about it, Old Jew woman?'
Run..
..run!
BAP
BAP
BAP
You said to the witness, 'to me, you are no different than those arrogant young nazis!'

'You religious types are so **blinkered** and **stubborn**, you start out believing in a god and you end up believing in the structure. The man-made structure. If your true God or messiah should suddenly arrive amongst us, you wouldn't believe it!'

'Around **God**, men form a shell of prayers and ceremonies and buildings and priests and rules and authority until God dies, and all you're left with are churches, smug and fattened on a bed of lies.'

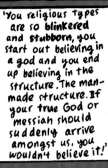

BAP

Shit.

The witness was **speechless.** It was a sunny day, poor kid.

I can hear popping noises from the house...strange..

eh!

!

You're in the street... not good, no house points here. You're not concentrating.

48

Next time they come, you're going to cut the crap quick and tell them you've met Jesus personally.

Did she see me?

You're angry at yourself for coming out of the house. This is very stupid.

No guns..

..no guns!

The panic in me is racing!

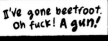

I've gone beetroot. Oh fuck! A gun!

You see an irritant. Not much time now. Have to leave girl, sort that out later. Never done this before but your father's words always stuck in your head. An opportunity arises. Forehead against nose bridge. Not forehead to forehead.

KRAK!

Instant disabling of opponent.

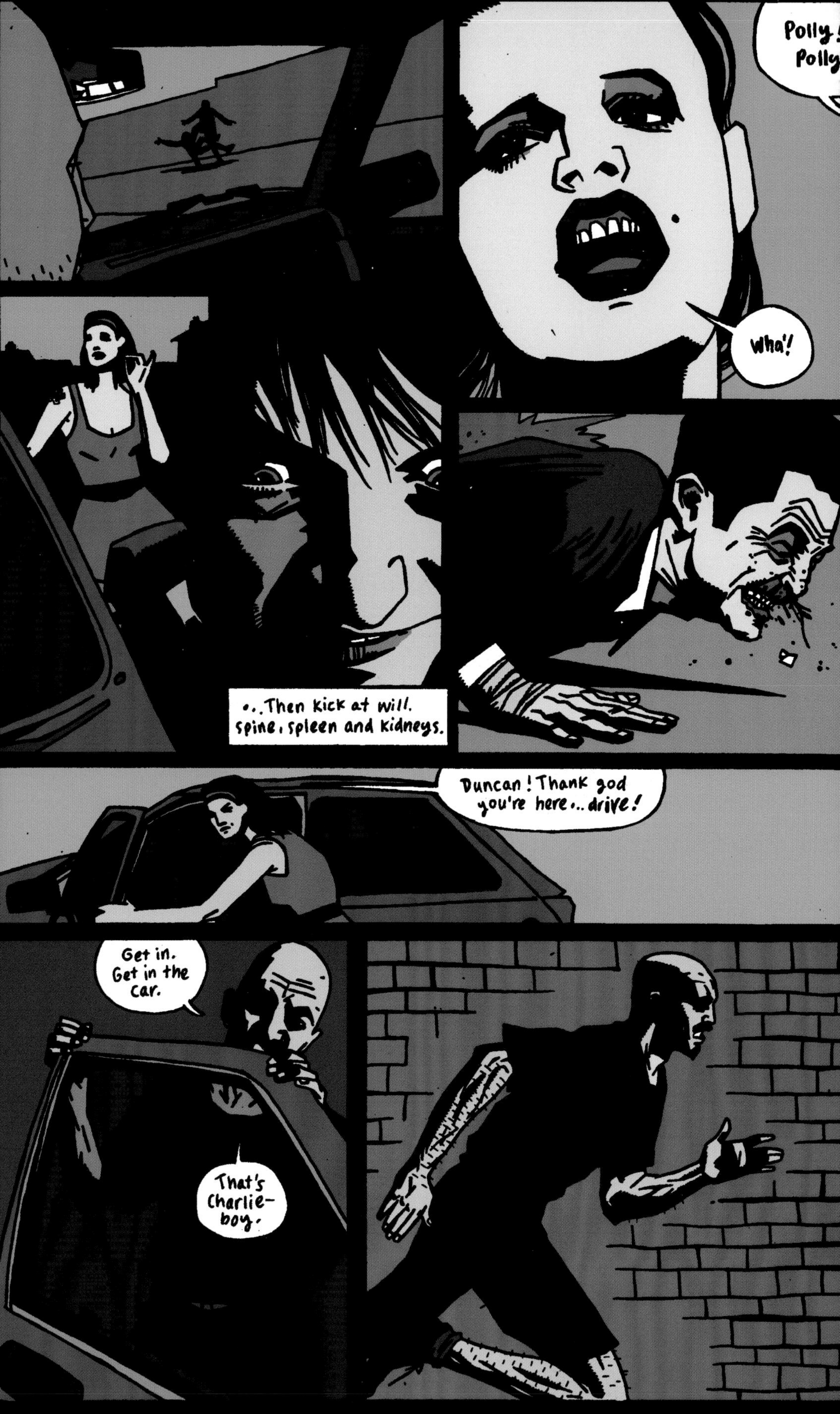
Polly! Polly
Wha'!
...Then kick at will. spine, spleen and kidneys.
Duncan! Thank god you're here...drive!
Get in. Get in the car.
That's Charlie-boy.

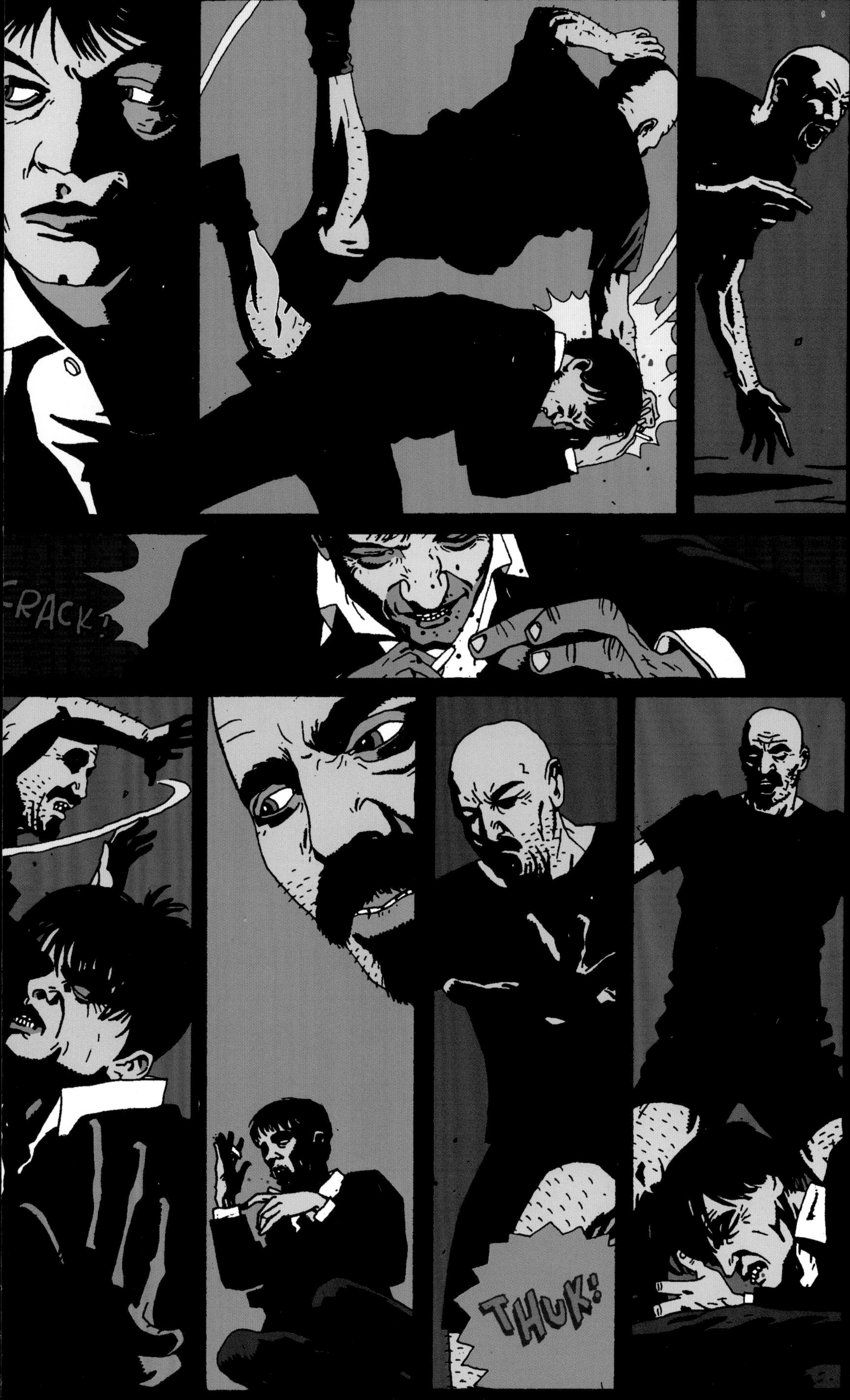
RACK!
THUK!

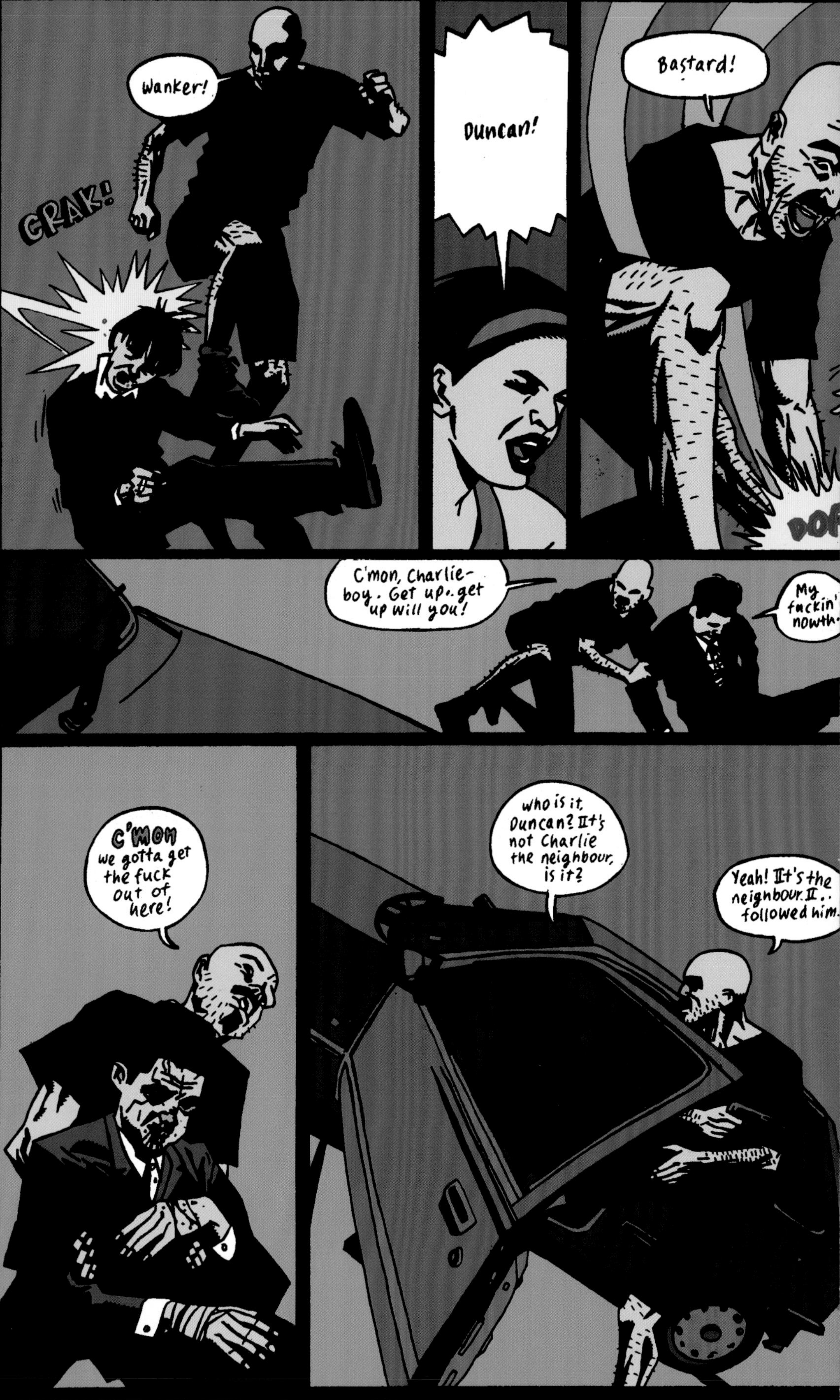
Wanker!
CRAK!
Duncan!
Bastard!
C'mon, Charlie-boy. Get up.. get up will you!
My fuckin' mouth-
C'MON we gotta get the fuck out of here!
who is it, Duncan? It's not Charlie the neighbour, is it?
Yeah! It's the neighbour. I.. followed him.

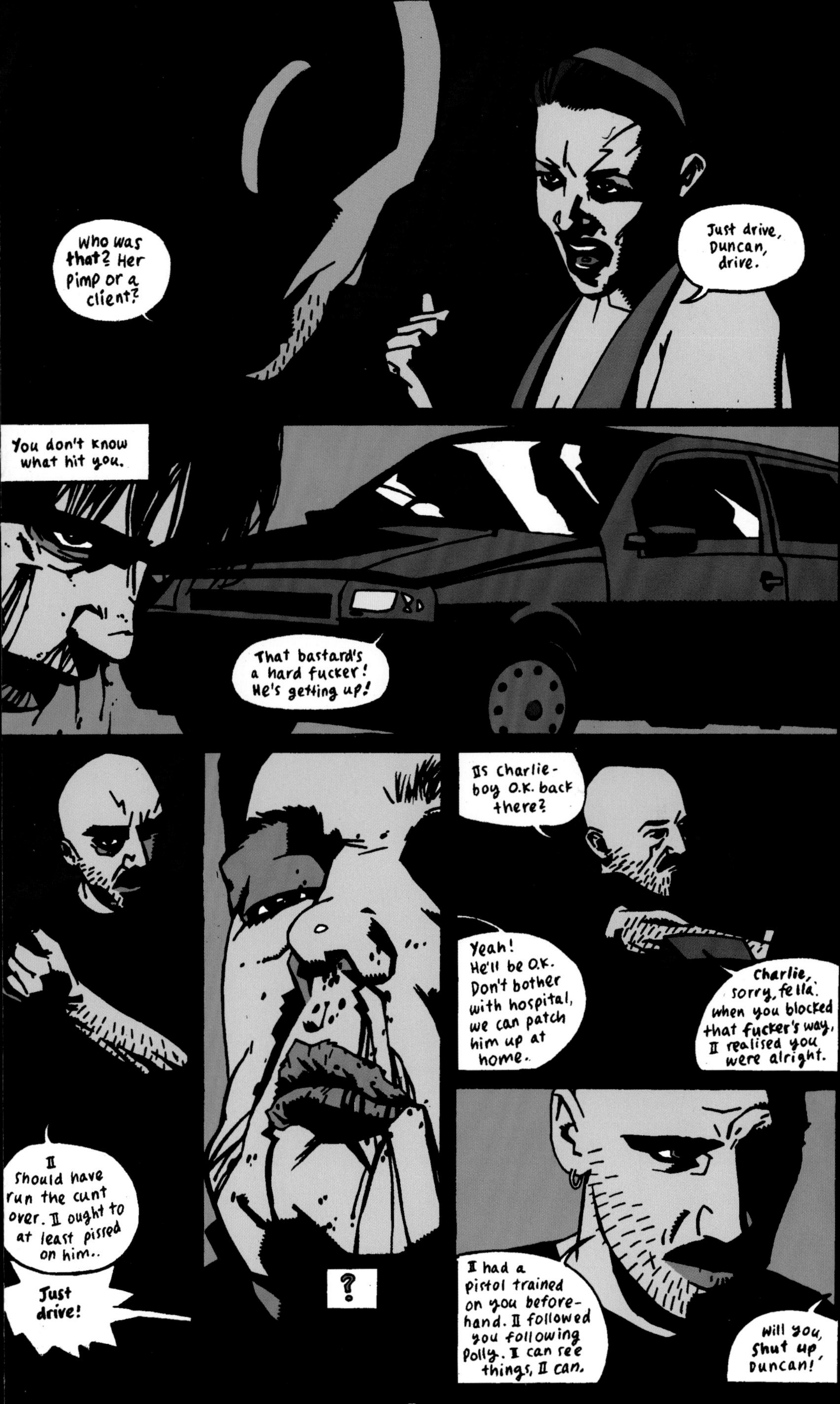
Who was that? Her pimp or a client?
Just drive, Duncan, drive.
You don't know what hit you.
That bastard's a hard fucker! He's getting up!
I should have run the cunt over. I ought to at least pissed on him..
Just drive!
?
Is Charlie-boy O.K. back there?
Yeah! He'll be O.K. Don't bother with hospital, we can patch him up at home.
Charlie, sorry, fella. when you blocked that fucker's way, I realised you were alright.
I had a pistol trained on you before-hand. I followed you following Polly. I can see things, I can.
Will you, shut up, Duncan!

Early this morning, a woman was found hanging in her flat. At this moment, we can reveal she was a prostitute.

At this moment, police haven't released her name. However, our sources suggest she was a prostitute known as 'Minty'.

We now hand over to Penny Fraser, live at the scene.. ..Penny..

I'm here at 23 Swans terrace with the chief investigating officer, inspector Raymond Croft.

Mr. Croft, is this a murder case or simply a suicide?

Suicide.

How long has she been hanging there? Was there a note?

She has been dead since the early hours of this morning, and yes, there was a suicide note.

This is certainly a suicide, yes!

This is Penny Fraser for the BBC breakfast news.

Thankyou, Penny..

Can you believe that? The poor cow gets knocked off and they fucking well call it suicide!.

..Maybe it's gang related.

Something bad's going on and now we've just got mixed up in it.

It's just like Cassy. She lived at your place, Charlie. She just upped and left. No warning... Killed herself in Leeds. And what about Mrs. Hitchens?

Tea anyone?

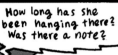

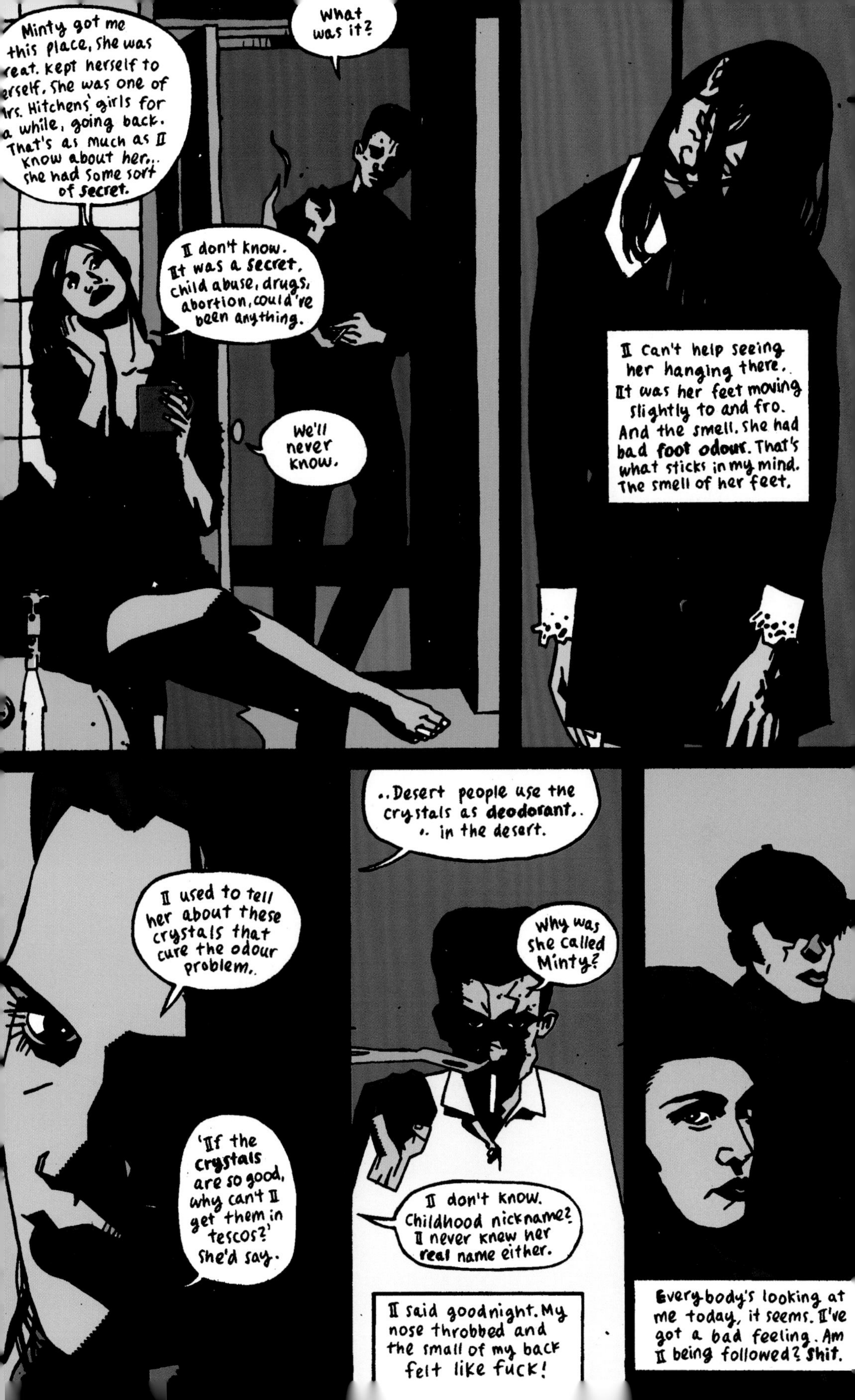

Minty got me this place, she was reat. kept herself to erself. She was one of rs. Hitchens' girls for a while, going back. That's as much as I know about her.. she had some sort of secret.
What was it?
I don't know. It was a secret, child abuse, drugs, abortion, could've been anything.
We'll never know.
I can't help seeing her hanging there. It was her feet moving slightly to and fro. And the smell. She had bad foot odour. That's what sticks in my mind. The smell of her feet.
I used to tell her about these crystals that cure the odour problem.
'If the crystals are so good, why can't I get them in tescos?' She'd say.
..Desert people use the crystals as deodorant.. .. in the desert.
Why was she called Minty?
I don't know. Childhood nickname? I never knew her real name either.
I said goodnight. My nose throbbed and the small of my back felt like fuck!
Everybody's looking at me today, it seems. I've got a bad feeling. Am I being followed? Shit.

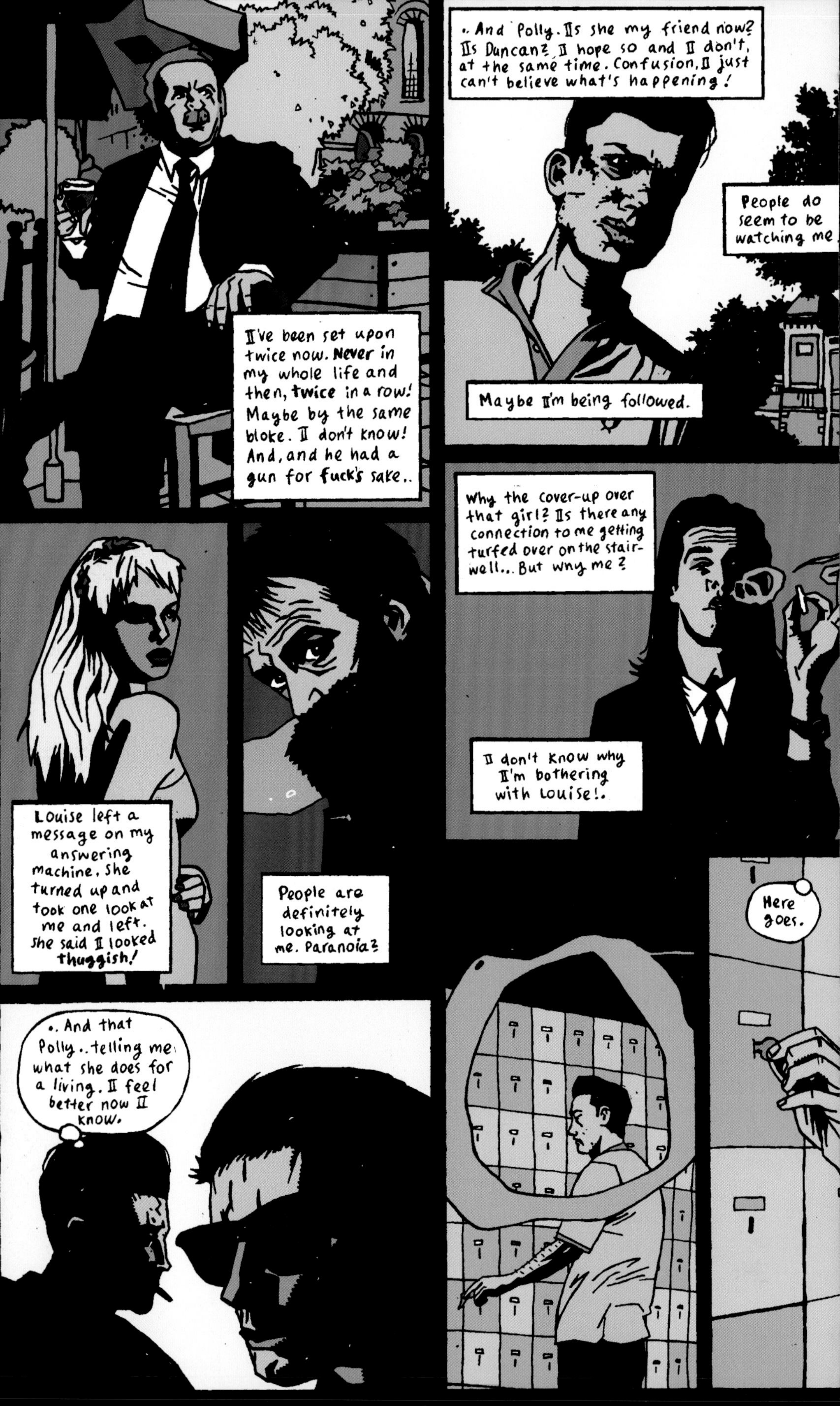
I've been set upon twice now. Never in my whole life and then, twice in a row! Maybe by the same bloke. I don't know! And, and he had a gun for fuck's sake..
.. And Polly. Is she my friend now? Is Duncan? I hope so and I don't, at the same time. Confusion, I just can't believe what's happening!
People do seem to be watching me.
Maybe I'm being followed.
Louise left a message on my answering machine. She turned up and took one look at me and left. She said I looked thuggish!
People are definitely looking at me. Paranoia?
Why the cover-up over that girl? Is there any connection to me getting turfed over on the stair-well... But why me?
I don't know why I'm bothering with Louise!.
.. And that Polly.. telling me what she does for a living. I feel better now I know.
Here goes.

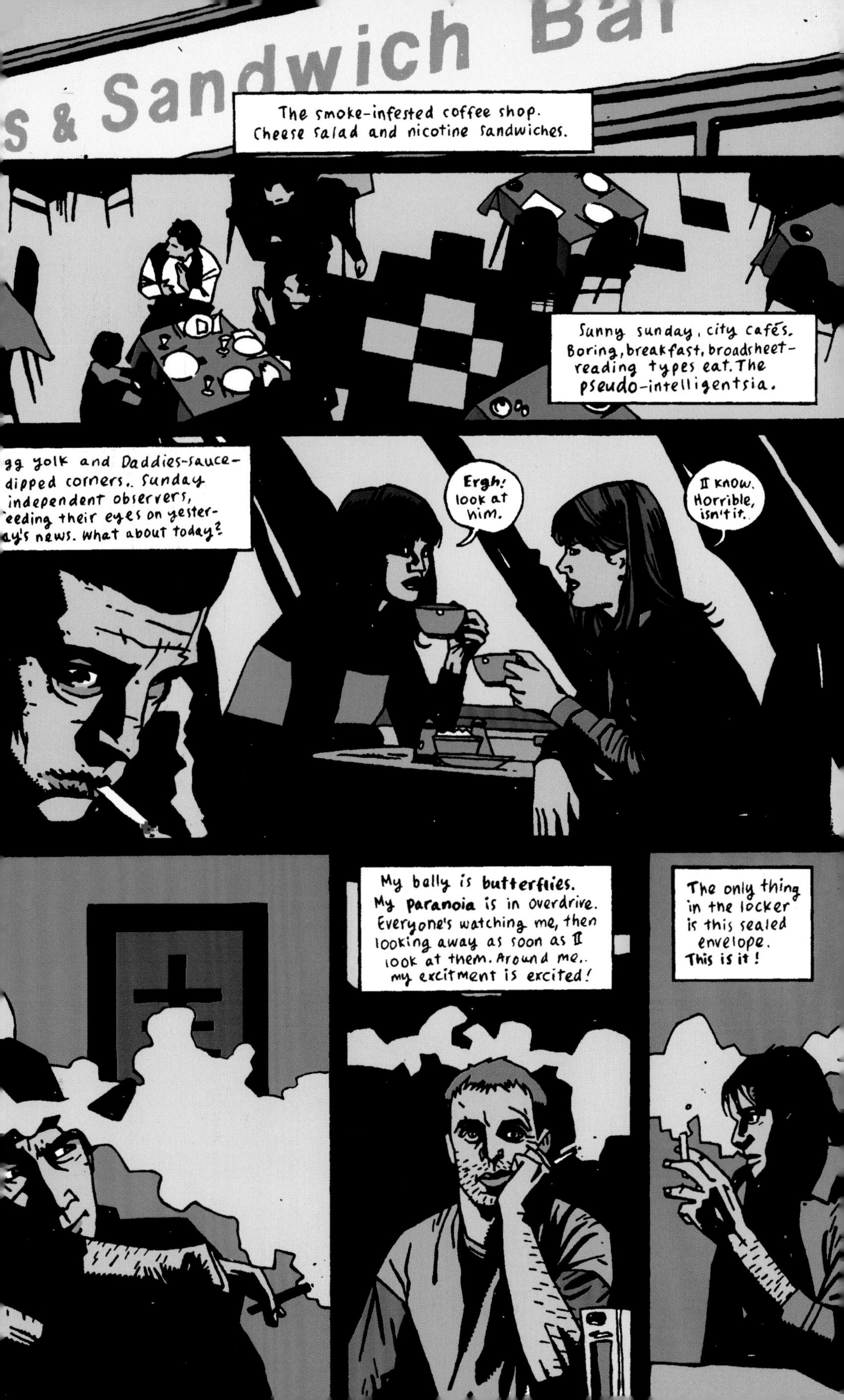

s & Sandwich Bar
The smoke-infested coffee shop. Cheese salad and nicotine sandwiches.
Sunny sunday, city cafés. Boring, breakfast, broadsheet-reading types eat. The pseudo-intelligentsia.
gg yolk and Daddies-sauce-dipped corners.. Sunday independent observers, eeding their eyes on yester-ay's news. What about today?
Ergh! look at him.
I know. Horrible, isn't it.
My belly is **butterflies.** My **paranoia** is in overdrive. Everyone's watching me, then looking away as soon as I look at them. Around me.. my excitment is excited!
The only thing in the locker is this sealed envelope. **This is it!**

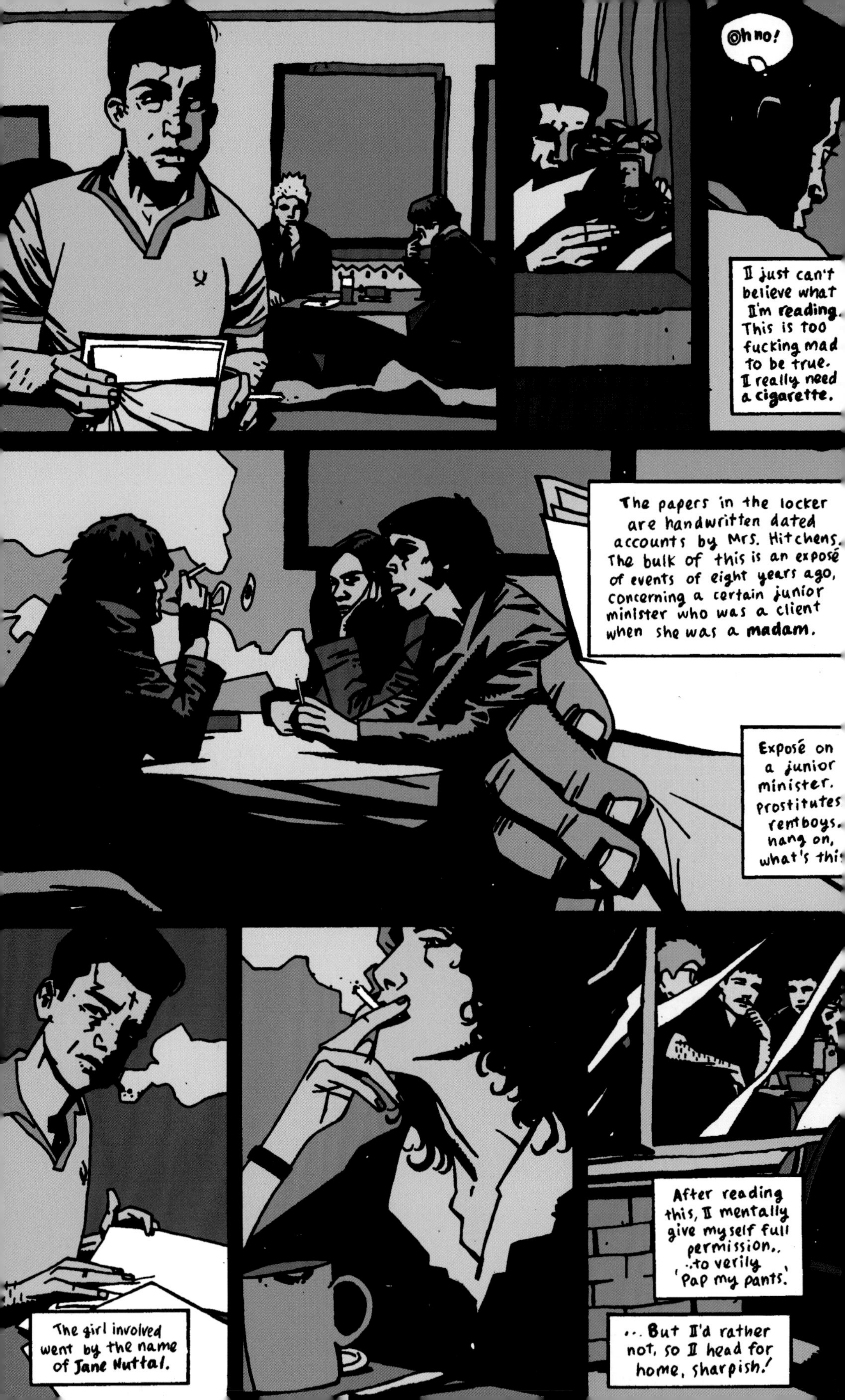
Oh no!
I just can't believe what I'm reading. This is too fucking mad to be true. I really need a cigarette.
The papers in the locker are handwritten dated accounts by Mrs. Hitchens. The bulk of this is an exposé of events of eight years ago, concerning a certain junior minister who was a client when she was a madam.
Exposé on a junior minister. Prostitutes rentboys. hang on, what's thi
The girl involved went by the name of Jane Nuttal.
After reading this, I mentally give myself full permission.. ..to verily 'Pap my pants.'
...But I'd rather not, so I head for home, sharpish!

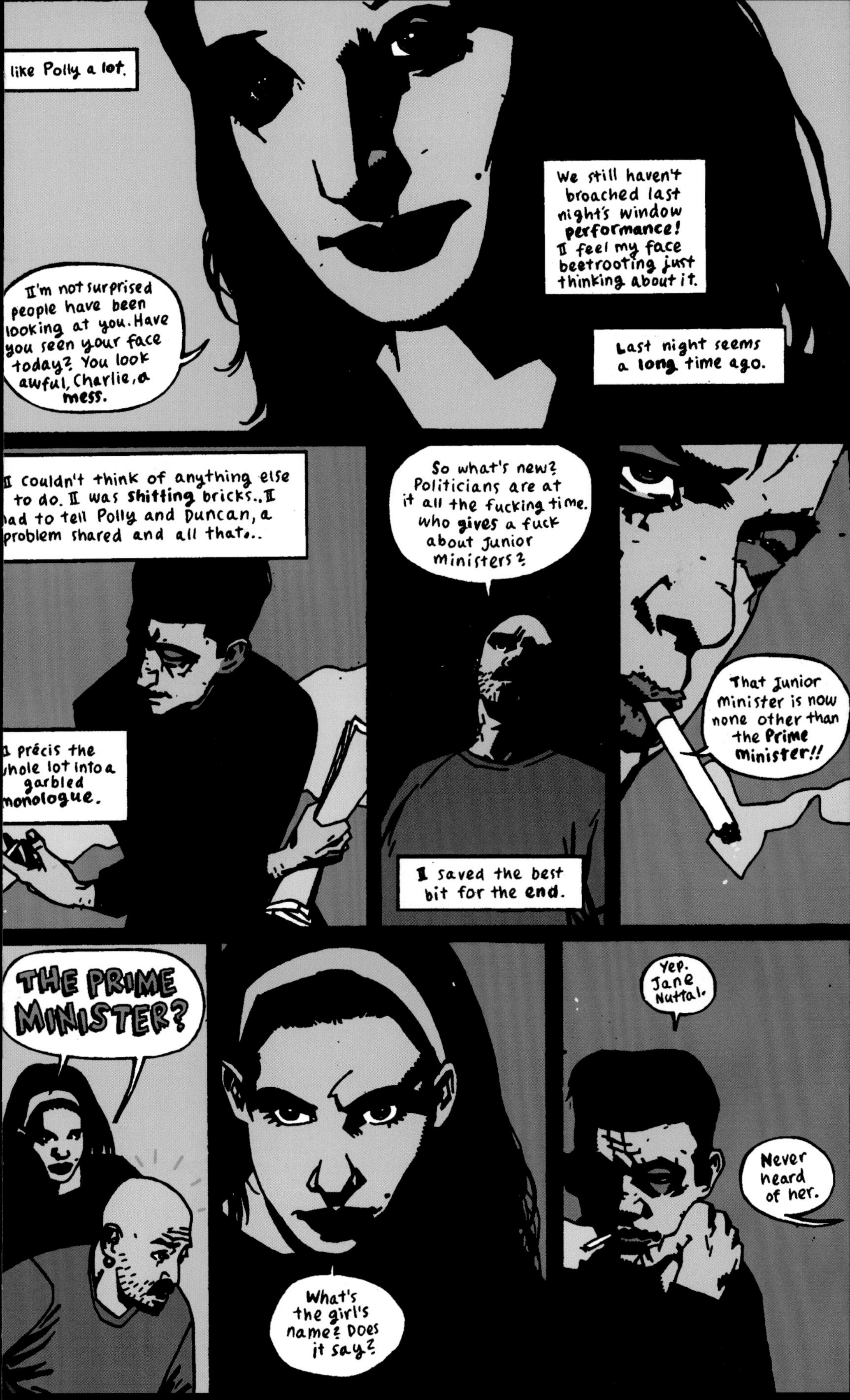
like Polly a lot.
We still haven't broached last night's window performance! I feel my face beetrooting just thinking about it.
I'm not surprised people have been looking at you. Have you seen your face today? You look awful, Charlie, a mess.
Last night seems a long time ago.
I couldn't think of anything else to do. I was shitting bricks.. I had to tell Polly and Duncan, a problem shared and all that..
précis the whole lot into a garbled monologue.
So what's new? Politicians are at it all the fucking time. Who gives a fuck about Junior Ministers?
I saved the best bit for the end.
That Junior minister is now none other than the Prime minister!!
THE PRIME MINISTER?
What's the girl's name? Does it say?
Yep. Jane Nuttal.
Never heard of her.

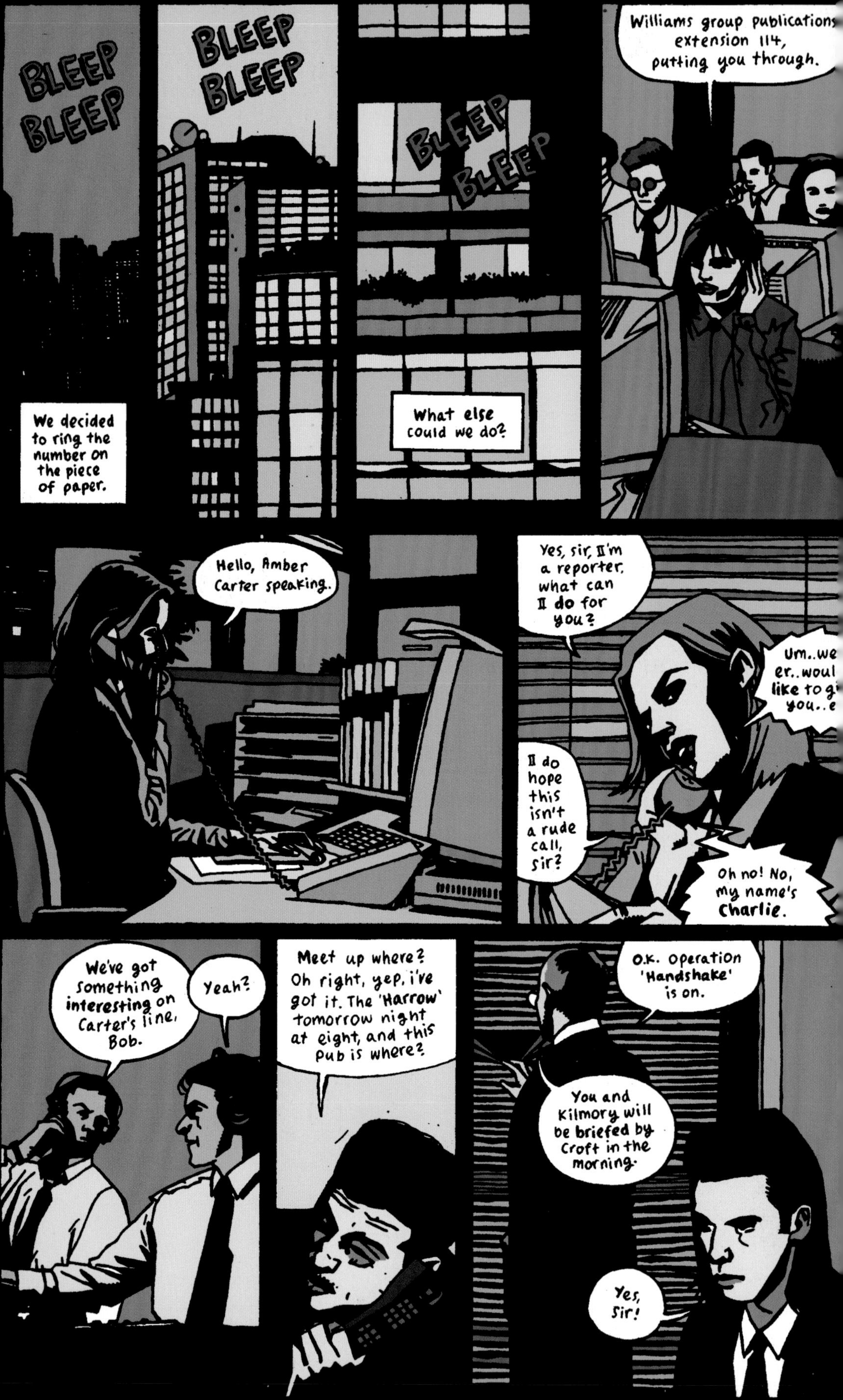

BLEEP BLEEP
We decided to ring the number on the piece of paper.
BLEEP BLEEP
BLEEP BLEEP
What else could we do?
Williams group publications extension 114, putting you through.
Hello, Amber Carter speaking.
Yes, sir, I'm a reporter. what can I do for you?
Um..we er..woul like to g you..e
I do hope this isn't a rude call, sir?
Oh no! No, my name's Charlie.
We've got something interesting on Carter's line, Bob.
Yeah?
Meet up where? Oh right, yep, i've got it. The 'Harrow' tomorrow night at eight, and this pub is where?
O.K. Operation 'Handshake' is on.
You and Kilmory will be briefed by Croft in the morning.
Yes, Sir!

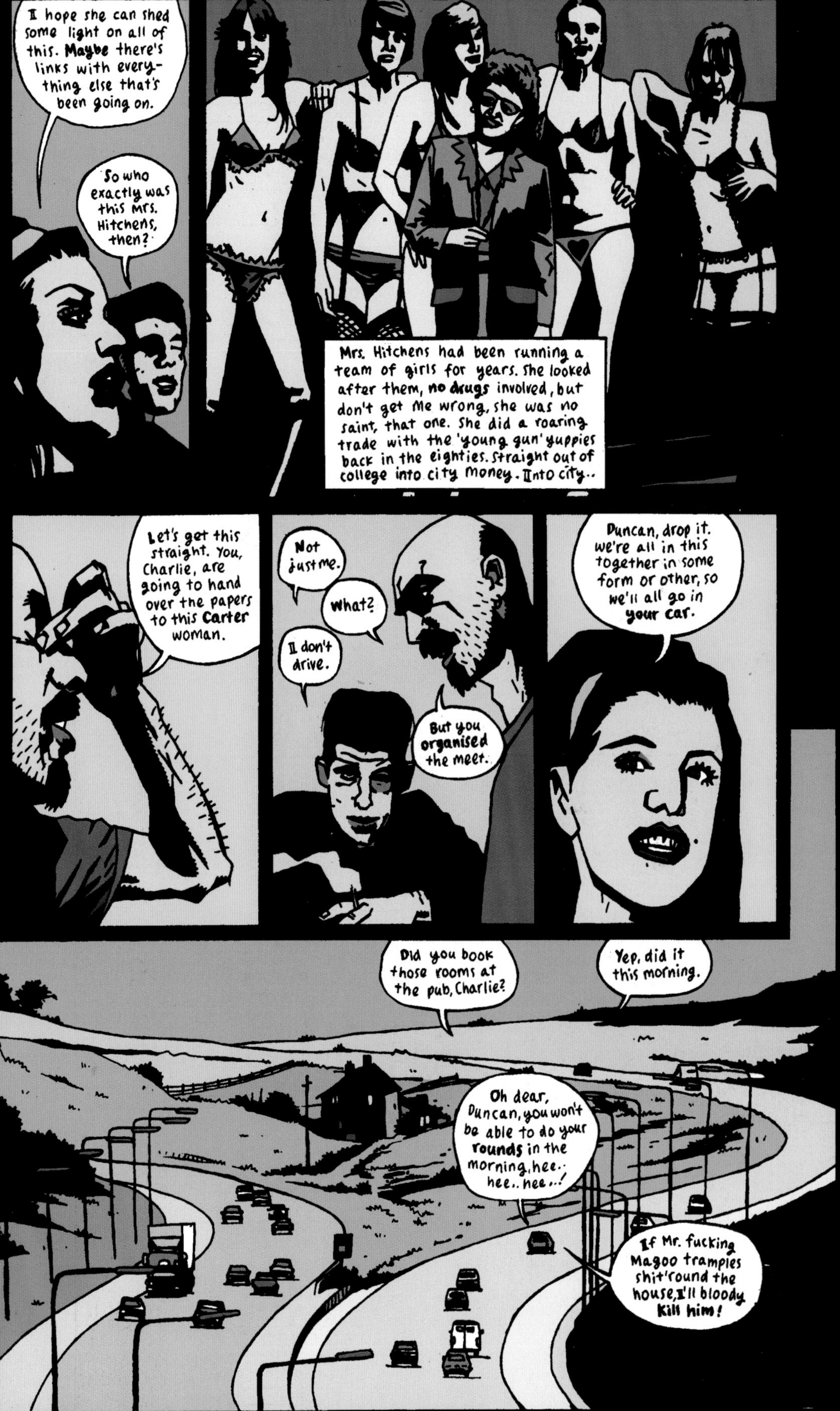
I hope she can shed some light on all of this. Maybe there's links with everything else that's been going on.
So who exactly was this Mrs. Hitchens, then?
Mrs. Hitchens had been running a team of girls for years. She looked after them, no drugs involved, but don't get me wrong, she was no saint, that one. She did a roaring trade with the 'young gun' yuppies back in the eighties. Straight out of college into city money. Into city..
Let's get this straight. You, Charlie, are going to hand over the papers to this Carter woman.
Not just me.
What?
I don't drive.
But you organised the meet.
Duncan, drop it. We're all in this together in some form or other, so we'll all go in your car.
Did you book those rooms at the pub, Charlie?
Yep, did it this morning.
Oh dear, Duncan, you won't be able to do your rounds in the morning, hee.. hee.. hee..!
If Mr. fucking Magoo tramples shit 'round the house, I'll bloody kill him!

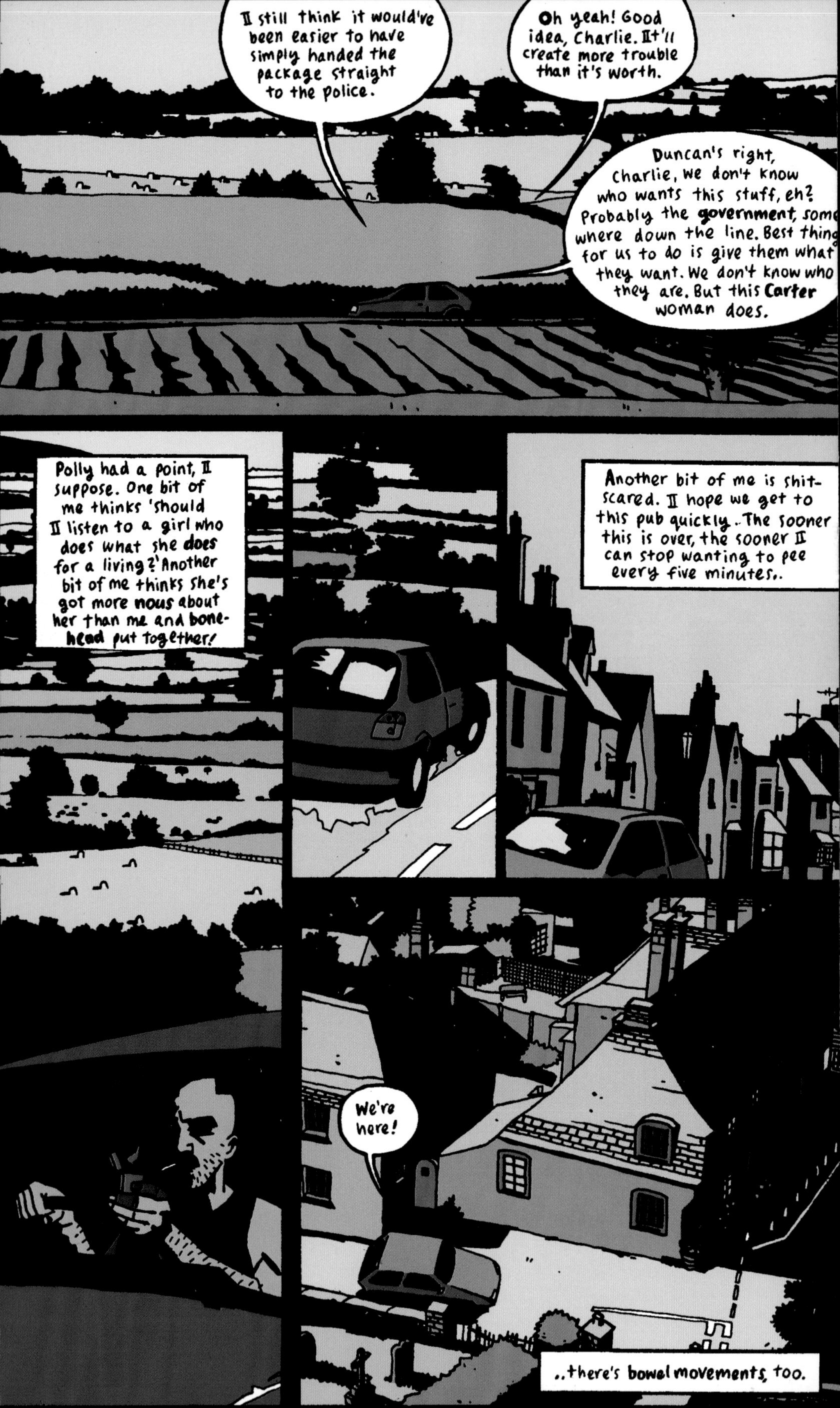
I still think it would've been easier to have simply handed the package straight to the police.
Oh yeah! Good idea, Charlie. It'll create more trouble than it's worth.
Duncan's right, Charlie, we don't know who wants this stuff, eh? Probably the government, some where down the line. Best thing for us to do is give them what they want. We don't know who they are. But this Carter woman does.
Polly had a point, I suppose. One bit of me thinks 'should I listen to a girl who does what she does for a living?' Another bit of me thinks she's got more nous about her than me and bonehead put together!
Another bit of me is shit-scared. I hope we get to this pub quickly.. The sooner this is over, the sooner I can stop wanting to pee every five minutes..
We're here!
..there's bowel movements, too.

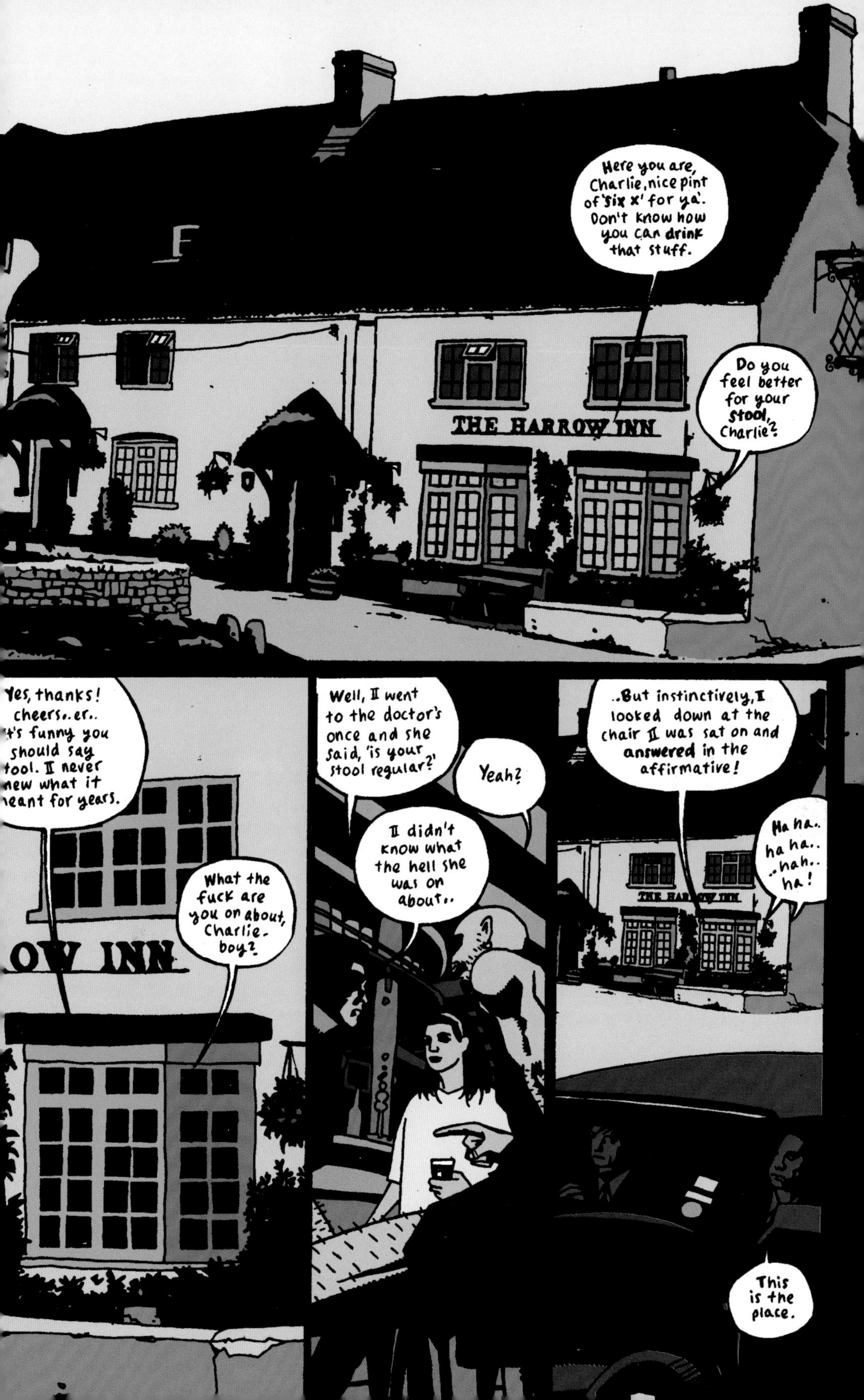
Here you are, Charlie, nice pint of 'Six X' for ya'. Don't know how you can drink that stuff.
Do you feel better for your stool, Charlie?
THE HARROW INN
Yes, thanks! cheers..er.. t's funny you should say tool. I never new what it neant for years.
What the fuck are you on about, Charlie-boy?
OW INN
Well, I went to the doctor's once and she said, 'is your stool regular?'
Yeah?
I didn't know what the hell she was on about..
..But instinctively, I looked down at the chair I was sat on and answered in the affirmative!
Ha ha.. ha ha.. ..hah.. ha!
THE HARROW INN
This is the place.

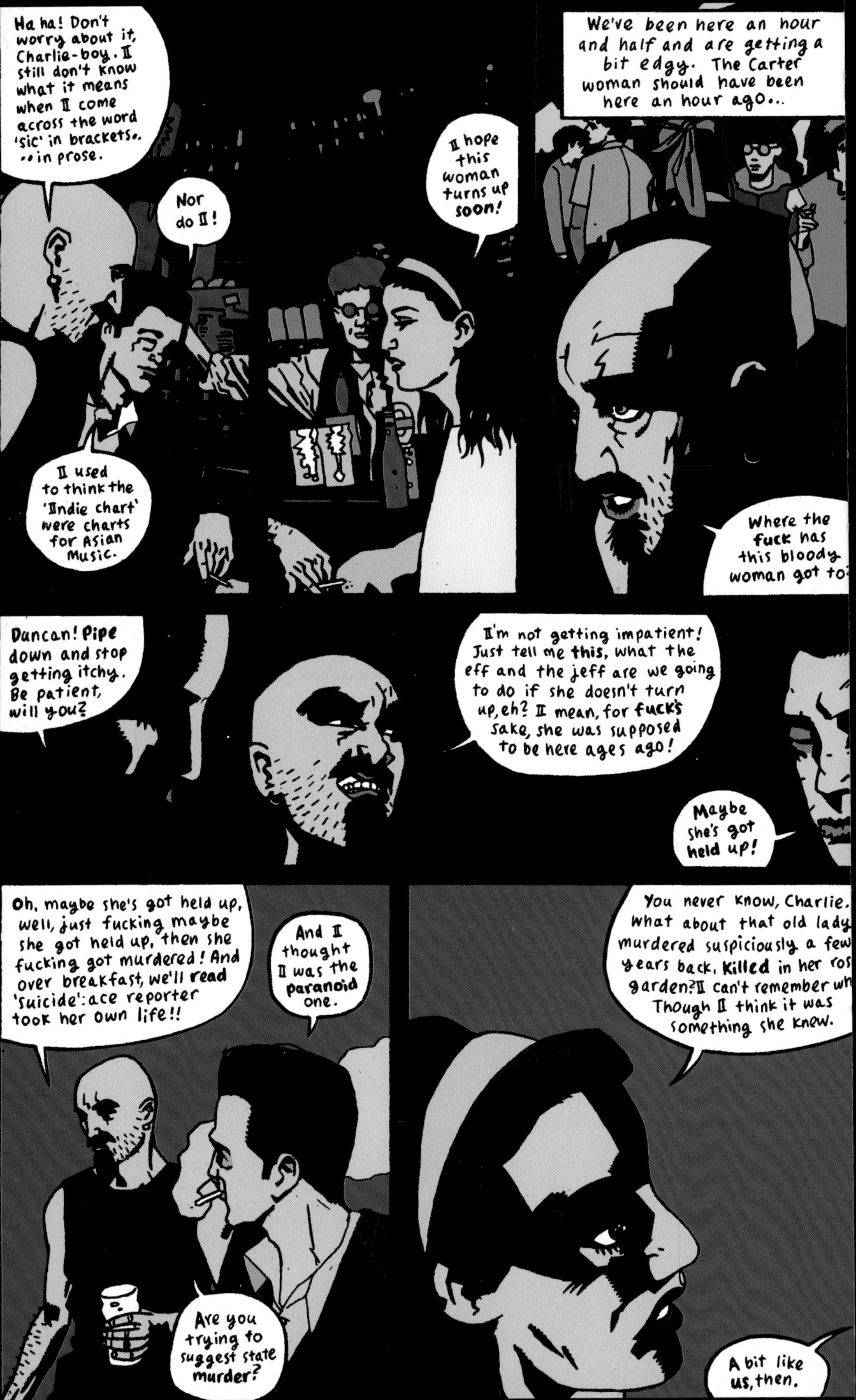

Ha ha! Don't worry about it, Charlie-boy. I still don't know what it means when I come across the word 'sic' in brackets.. ..in prose.
Nor do I!
I used to think the 'Indie chart' were charts for Asian music.
I hope this woman turns up soon!
We've been here an hour and half and are getting a bit edgy. The Carter woman should have been here an hour ago..
Where the fuck has this bloody woman got to?
Duncan! Pipe down and stop getting itchy. Be patient, will you?
I'm not getting impatient! Just tell me this, what the eff and the jeff are we going to do if she doesn't turn up, eh? I mean, for fuck's sake, she was supposed to be here ages ago!
Maybe she's got held up!
Oh, maybe she's got held up, well, just fucking maybe she got held up, then she fucking got murdered! And over breakfast, we'll read 'suicide': ace reporter took her own life!!
And I thought I was the paranoid one.
Are you trying to suggest state murder?
You never know, Charlie. What about that old lady murdered suspiciously a few years back. Killed in her ros garden? I can't remember wh Though I think it was something she knew.
A bit like us, then.

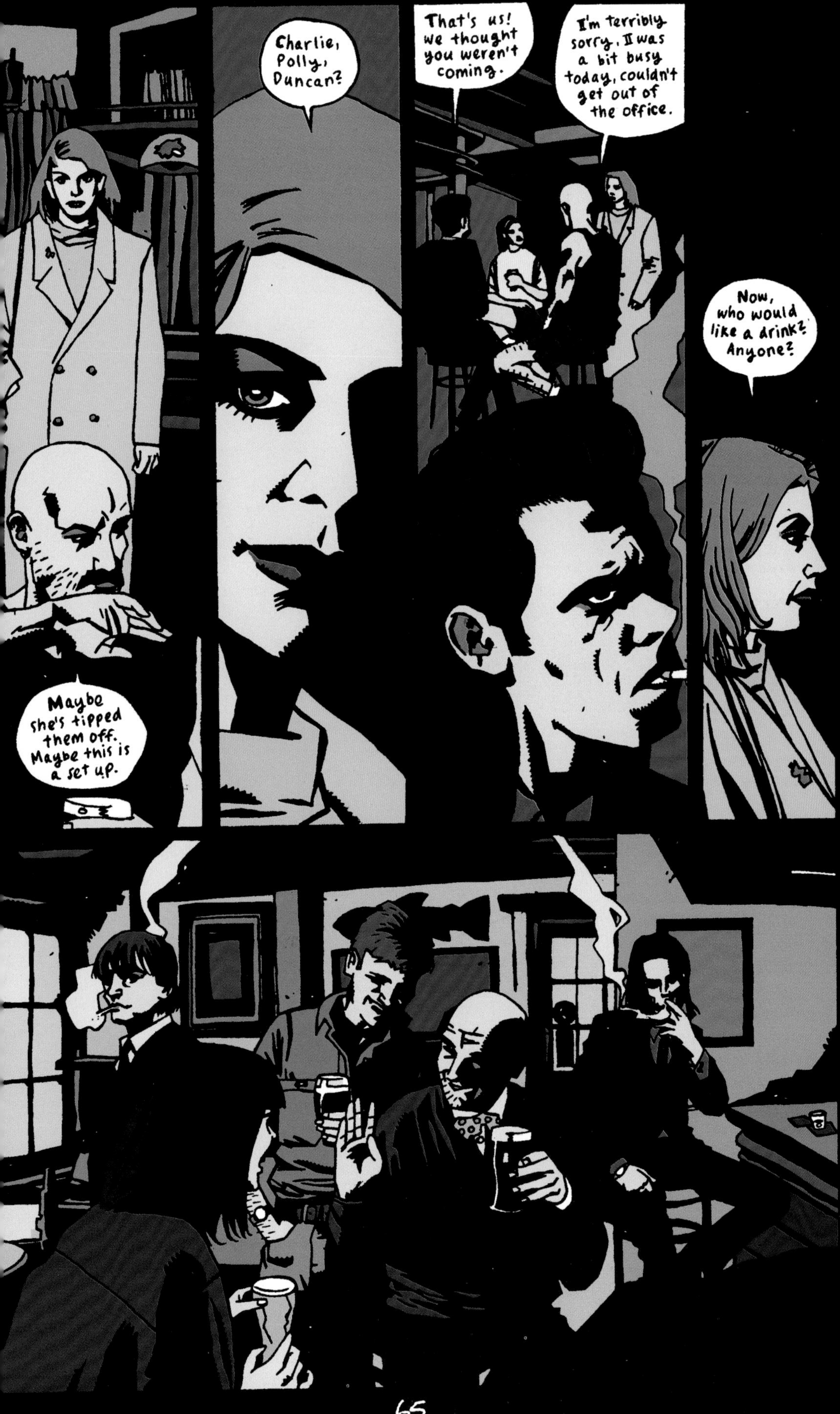
Maybe she's tipped them off. Maybe this is a set up.
Charlie, Polly, Duncan?
That's us! we thought you weren't coming.
I'm terribly sorry. I was a bit busy today, couldn't get out of the office.
Now, who would like a drink? Anyone?

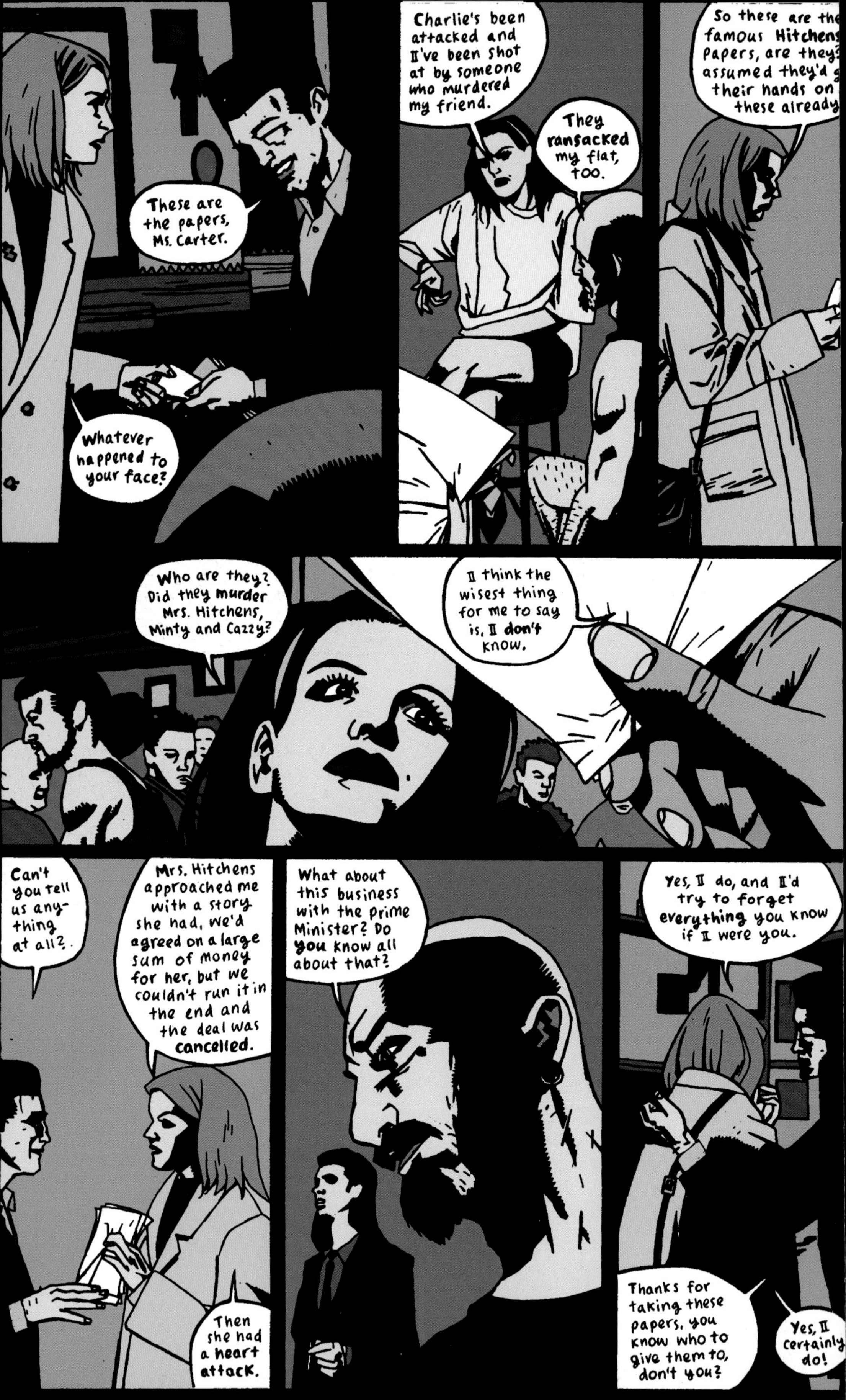
These are the papers, Ms. Carter.
Whatever happened to your face?
Charlie's been attacked and I've been shot at by someone who murdered my friend.
They ransacked my flat, too.
So these are the famous Hitchens papers, are they? assumed they'd g their hands on these already
Who are they? Did they murder Mrs. Hitchens, Minty and Cazzy?
I think the wisest thing for me to say is, I don't know.
Can't you tell us any-thing at all?
Mrs. Hitchens approached me with a story she had, we'd agreed on a large sum of money for her, but we couldn't run it in the end and the deal was cancelled.
Then she had a heart attack.
What about this business with the prime Minister? Do you know all about that?
Yes, I do, and I'd try to forget everything you know if I were you.
Thanks for taking these papers, you know who to give them to, don't you?
Yes, I certainly do!

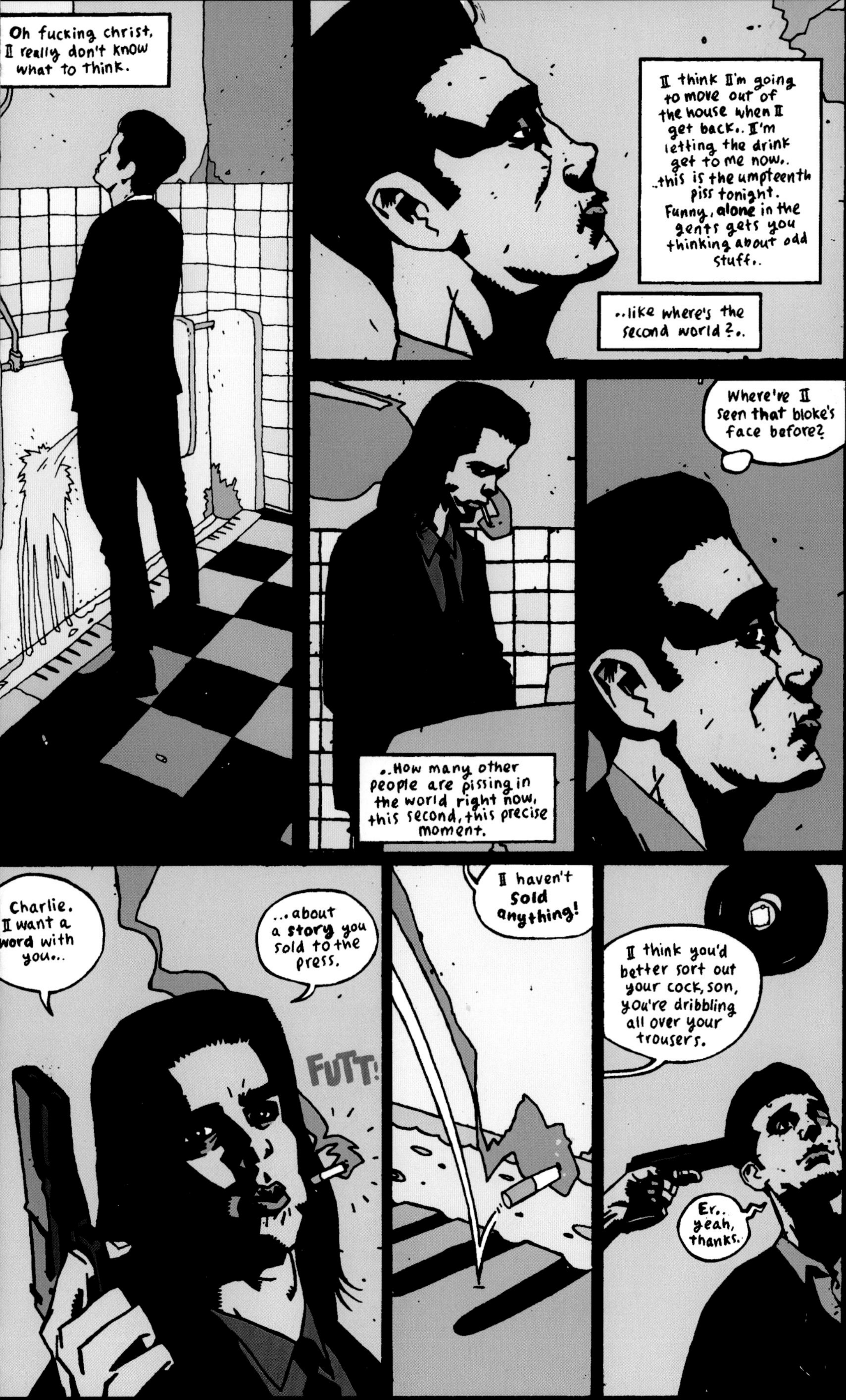

Oh fucking christ, I really don't know what to think.
I think I'm going to move out of the house when I get back.. I'm letting the drink get to me now.. ..this is the umpteenth piss tonight. Funny, alone in the gents gets you thinking about odd stuff..
..like where's the second world?..
Where're I seen that bloke's face before?
..How many other people are pissing in the world right now, this second, this precise moment.
Charlie. I want a word with you..
...about a story you sold to the press.
FUTT!
I haven't sold anything!
I think you'd better sort out your cock, son, you're dribbling all over your trousers.
Er.. yeah, thanks.

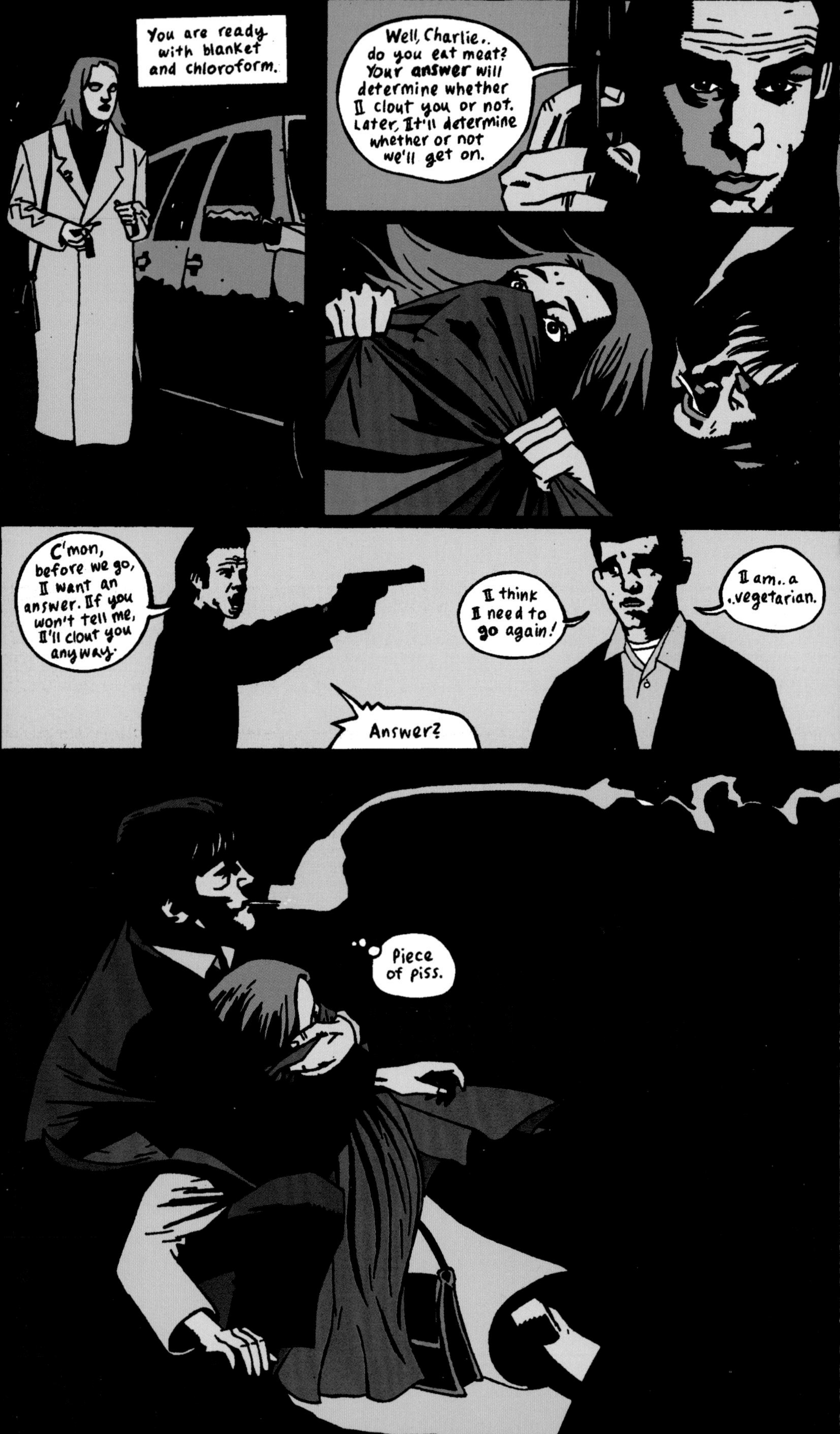
You are ready with blanket and chloroform.
Well, Charlie.. do you eat meat? Your answer will determine whether I clout you or not. Later, It'll determine whether or not we'll get on.
C'mon, before we go, I want an answer. If you won't tell me, I'll clout you anyway.
I think I need to go again!
I am.. a ..vegetarian.
Answer?
Piece of piss.

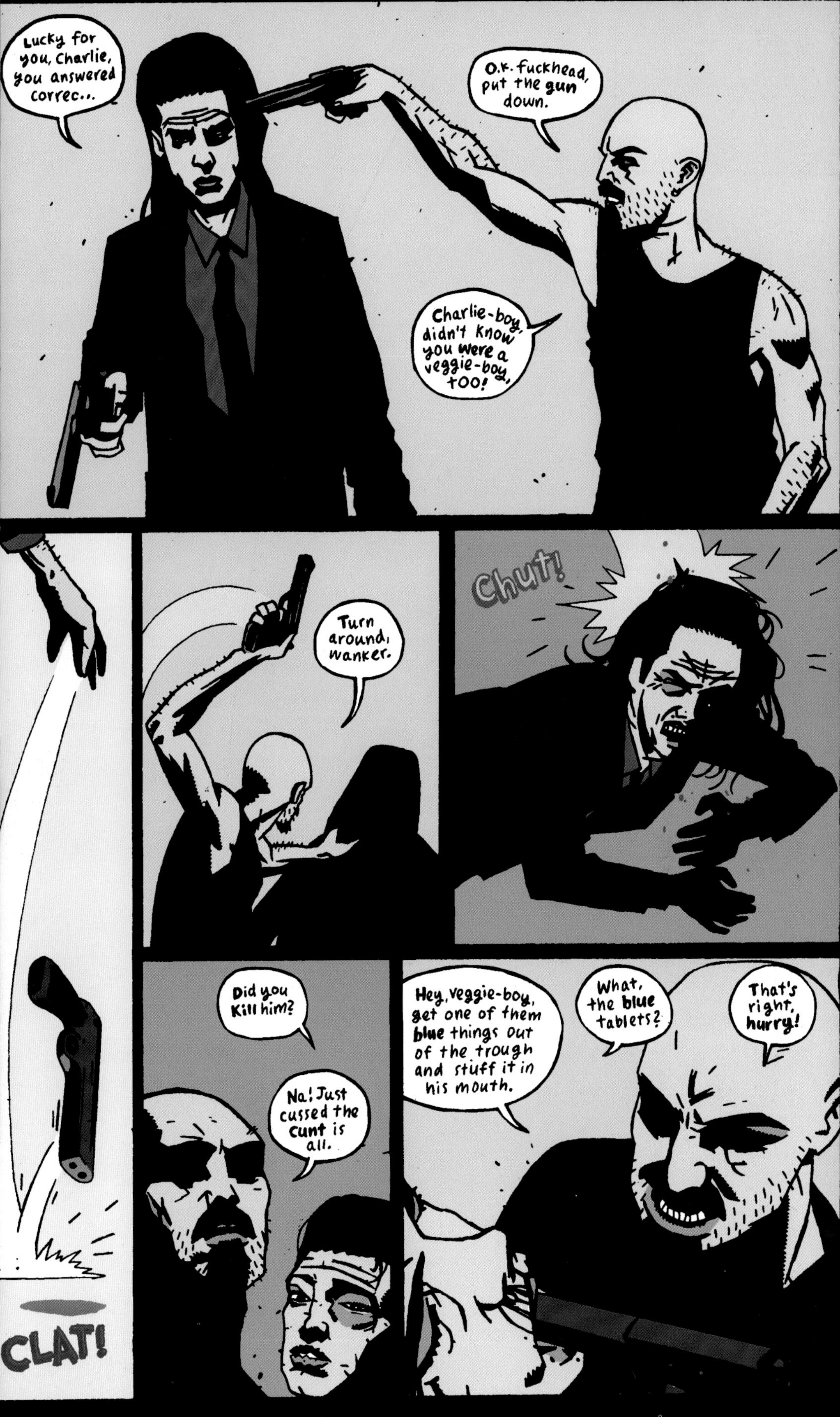
Lucky for you, Charlie, you answered correc...
O.K. fuckhead, put the gun down.
Charlie-boy, didn't know you were a veggie-boy, too!
Turn around, wanker.
Chut!
CLAT!
Did you kill him?
Na! Just cussed the cunt is all.
Hey, veggie-boy, get one of them blue things out of the trough and stuff it in his mouth.
What, the blue tablets?
That's right, hurry!

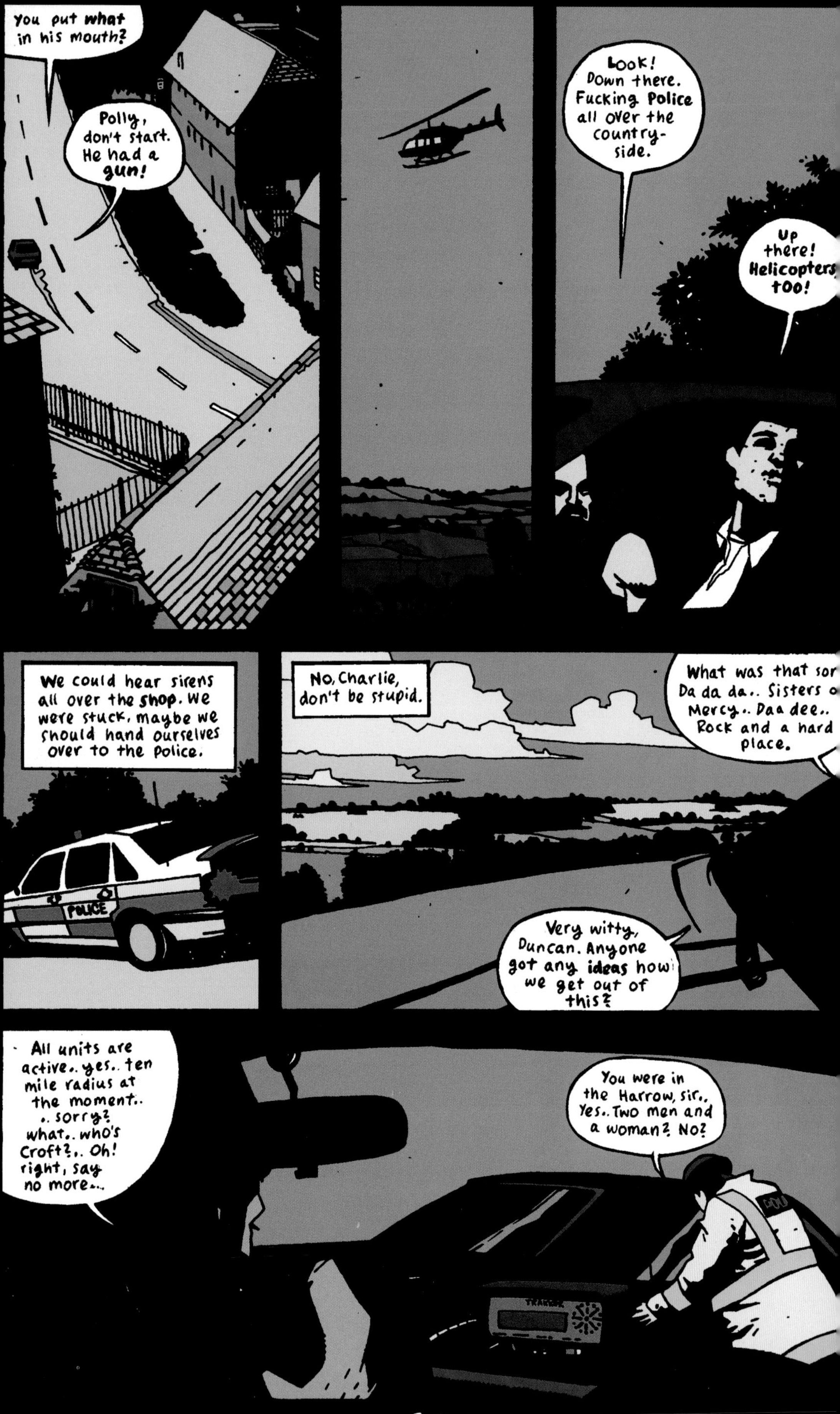
You put what in his mouth?
Polly, don't start. He had a gun!
Look! Down there. Fucking Police all over the country-side.
Up there! Helicopters too!
We could hear sirens all over the shop. We were stuck, maybe we should hand ourselves over to the police.
POLICE
No, Charlie, don't be stupid.
What was that sor
Da da da.. Sisters o
Mercy.. Daa dee..
Rock and a hard
place.
Very witty, Duncan. Anyone got any ideas how we get out of this?
All units are active.. yes.. ten mile radius at the moment.. .. sorry? what.. who's Croft?.. Oh! right, say no more...
You were in the Harrow, sir.. Yes.. Two men and a woman? No?

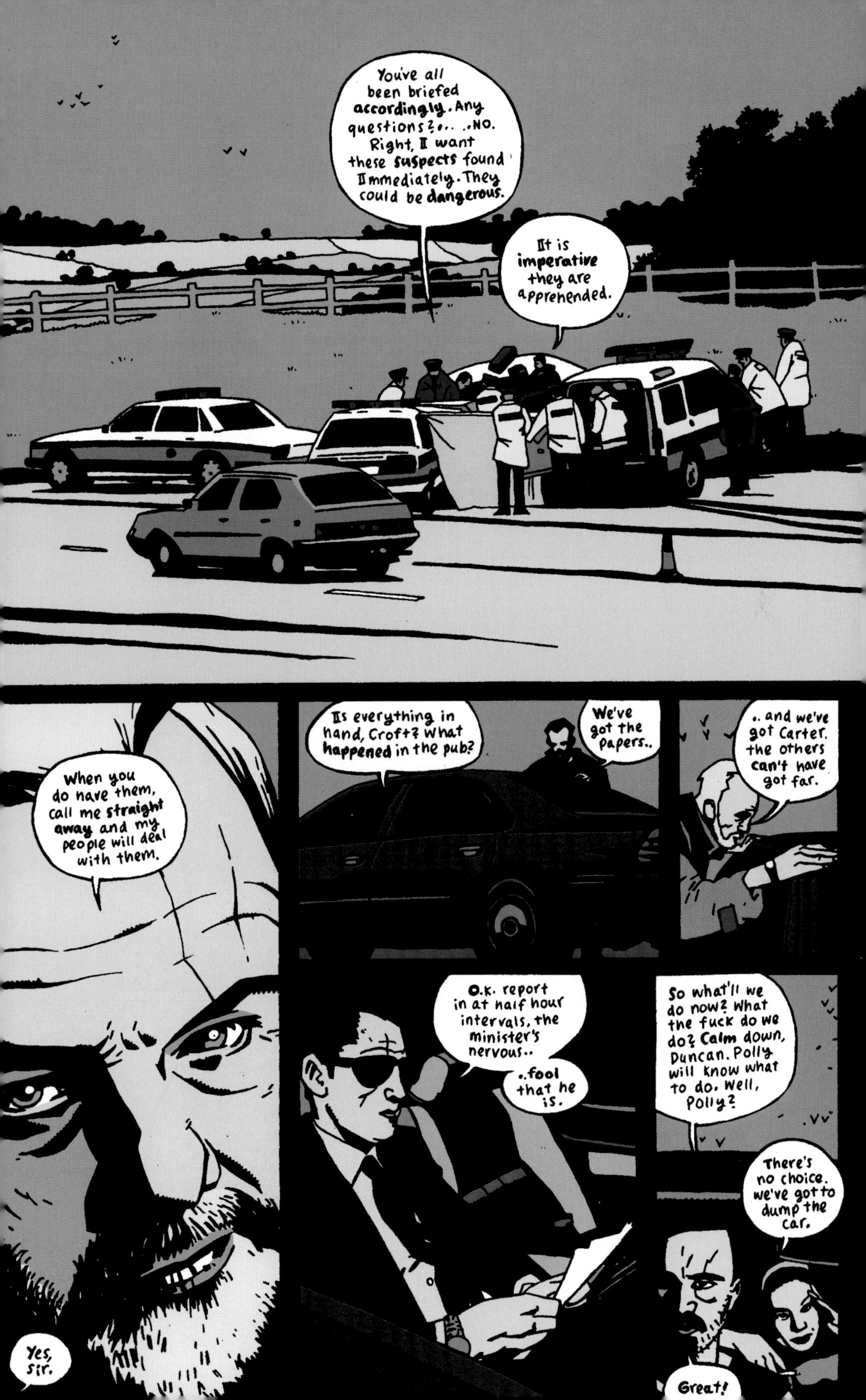
You've all been briefed accordingly. Any questions?... ..NO. Right, I want these suspects found Immediately. They could be dangerous.
It is imperative they are apprenended.
When you do have them, call me straight away and my people will deal with them.
Yes, sir.
Is everything in hand, Croft? What happened in the pub?
We've got the papers..
.. and we've got Carter. the others can't have got far.
O.K. report in at half hour intervals, the minister's nervous..
..fool that he is.
So what'll we do now? What the fuck do we do? Calm down, Duncan. Polly will know what to do. Well, Polly?
There's no choice. we've got to dump the car.
Great!

I can't get this **fucking** taste out of my mouth.

Quit moaning, man, there's toothpaste in the car.

Where's Kilmory & Fenelon? .Well, tell th to get th arses ove here quic

Don't worry, veggie-boy, Polly knows some people who might be able to help us.

Can someone tell me what we're going to do? Duncan?

Calm down, Charlie, we've just got to find somewhere to sleep tonight!

Right, you two. I've got a team on standby in the woods. I want you **both** with them.

I'll have dropped there. Pl 'E', lads

We're on it, sir.

What about Carter?

Leave her with us.

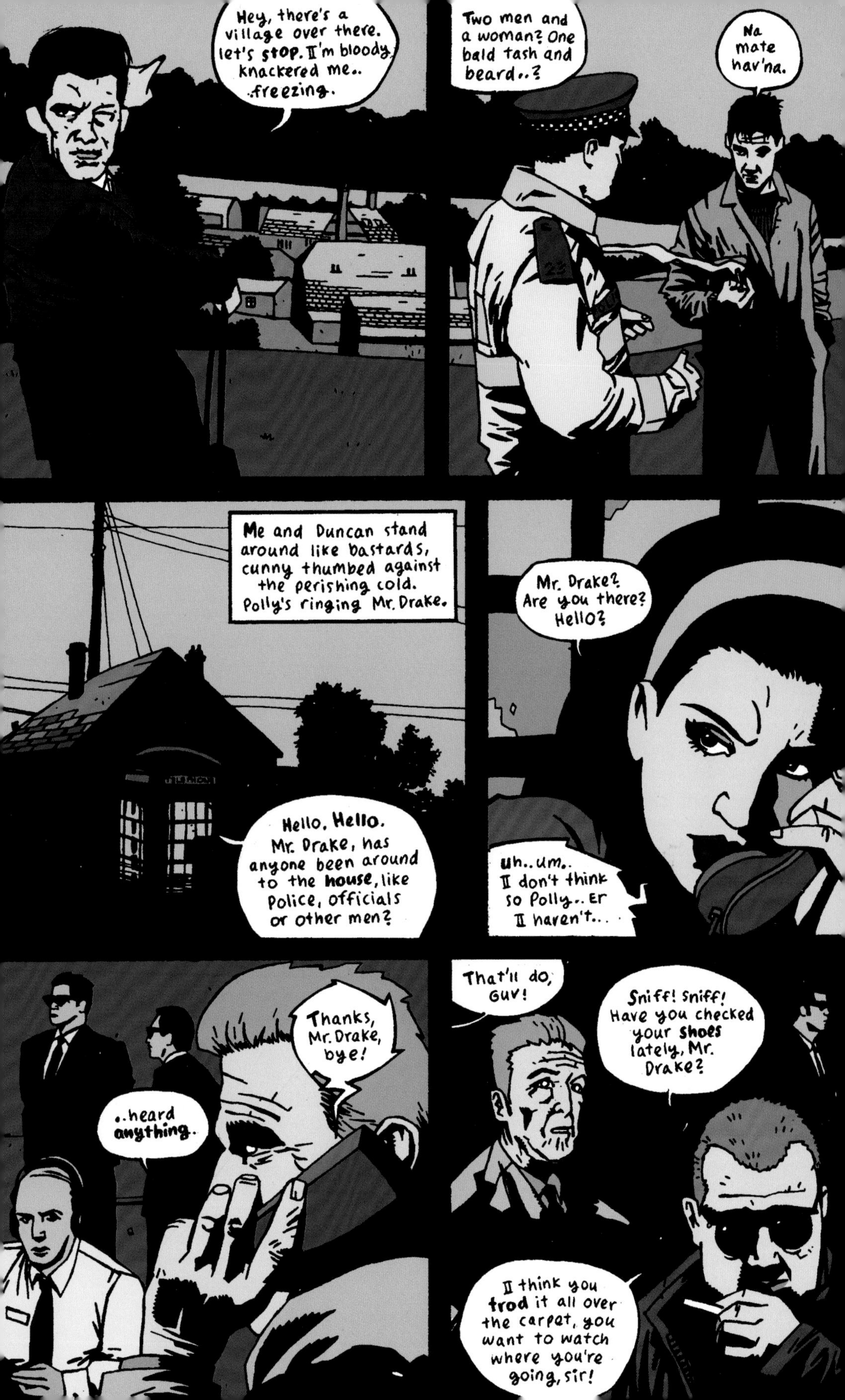
Hey, there's a village over there. let's stop. I'm bloody knackered me.. .freezing.
Two men and a woman? One bald tash and beard..?
Na mate hav'na.
Me and Duncan stand around like bastards, cunny thumbed against the perishing cold. Polly's ringing Mr. Drake.
Hello. Hello. Mr. Drake, has anyone been around to the house, like Police, officials or other men?
Mr. Drake? Are you there? Hello?
uh..um.. I don't think so Polly.. Er I haven't...
..heard anything.
Thanks, Mr. Drake, bye!
That'll do, Guv!
Sniff! sniff! Have you checked your shoes lately, Mr. Drake?
I think you trod it all over the carpet, you want to watch where you're going, sir!

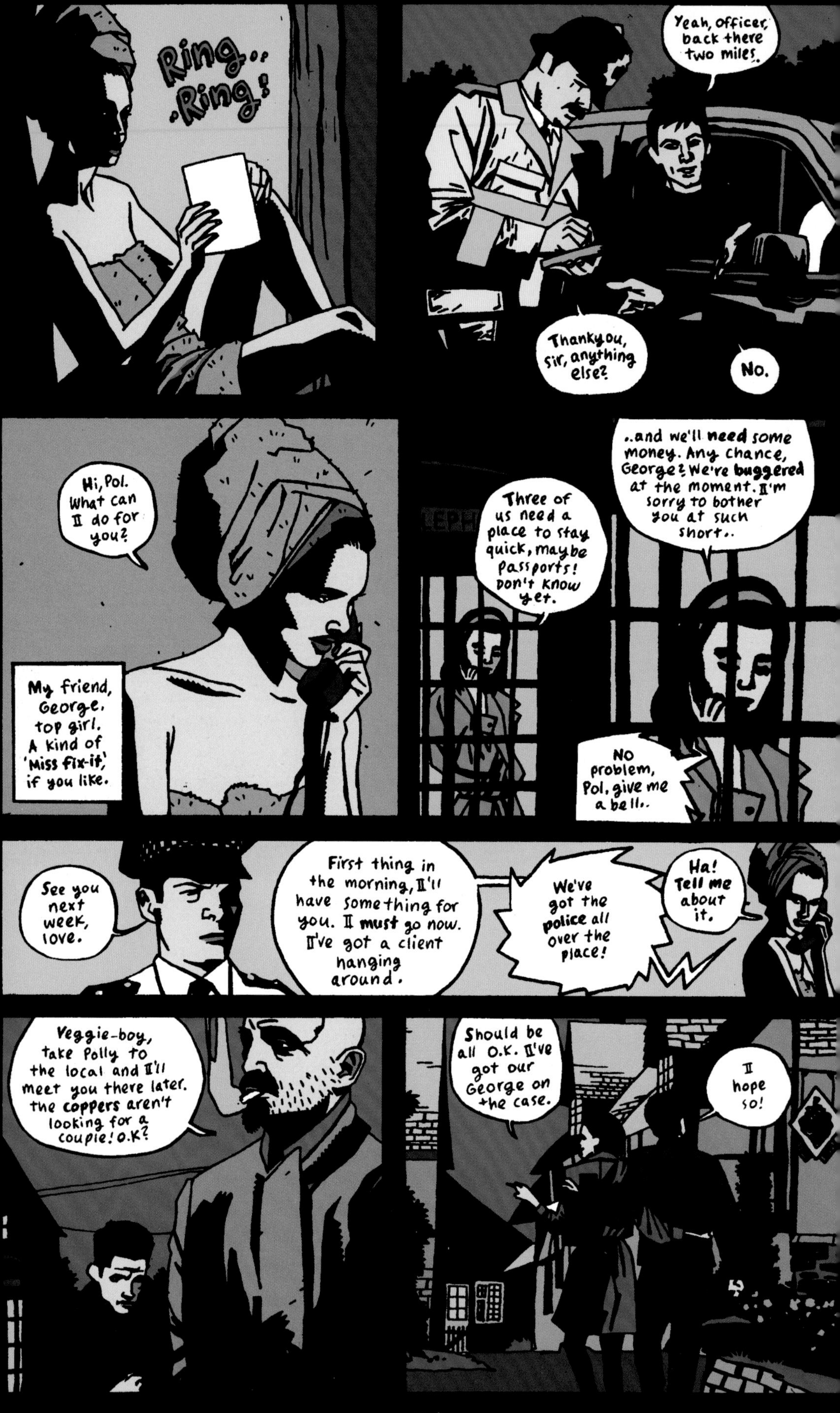
Ring.. .Ring!
Yeah, officer, back there two miles.
Thankyou, sir, anything else?
No.
Hi, Pol. What can I do for you?
My friend, George. top girl. A kind of 'Miss fix-it,' if you like.
Three of us need a place to stay quick, maybe passports! Don't know yet.
..and we'll need some money. Any chance, George? We're buggered at the moment. I'm sorry to bother you at such short..
No problem, Pol, give me a bell..
See you next week, love.
First thing in the morning, I'll have something for you. I must go now. I've got a client hanging around.
We've got the police all over the place!
Ha! Tell me about it.
Veggie-boy, take Polly to the local and I'll meet you there later. the coppers aren't looking for a couple! O.K?
Should be all O.K. I've got our George on the case.
I hope so!

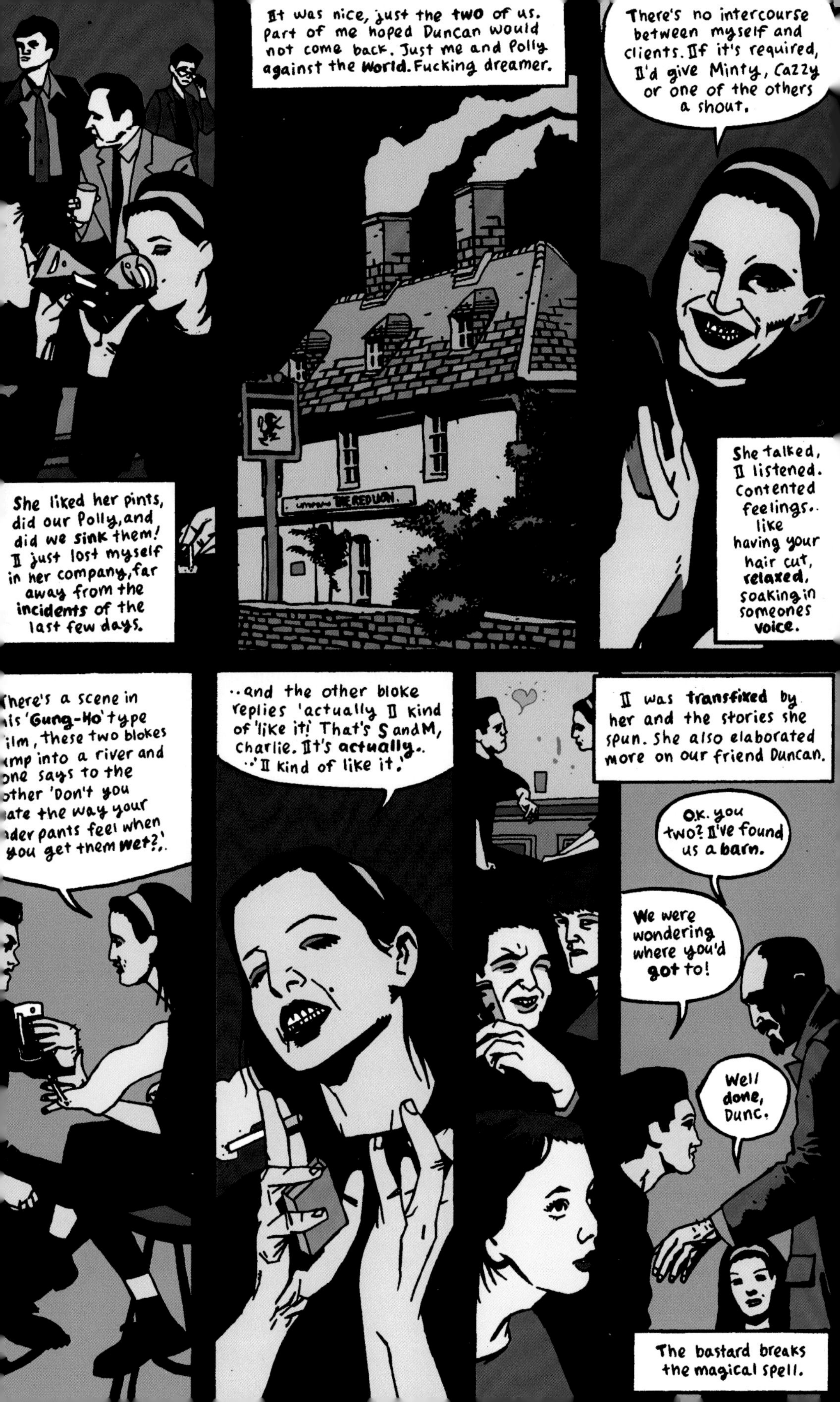

She liked her pints, did our Polly, and did we sink them! I just lost myself in her company, far away from the incidents of the last few days.
It was nice, just the two of us. Part of me hoped Duncan would not come back. Just me and Polly against the world. Fucking dreamer.
THE RED LION
There's no intercourse between myself and clients. If it's required, I'd give Minty, Cazzy or one of the others a shout.
She talked, I listened. Contented feelings.. like having your hair cut, relaxed, soaking in someones voice.
here's a scene in is 'Gung-Ho' type ilm, these two blokes mp into a river and one says to the other 'Don't you ate the way your der pants feel when you get them wet?'..
..and the other bloke replies 'actually I kind of 'like it'. That's S and M, Charlie. It's actually.. ..'I kind of like it.'
I was transfixed by her and the stories she spun. She also elaborated more on our friend Duncan.
O.K. you two? I've found us a barn.
We were wondering where you'd got to!
Well done, Dunc.
The bastard breaks the magical spell.

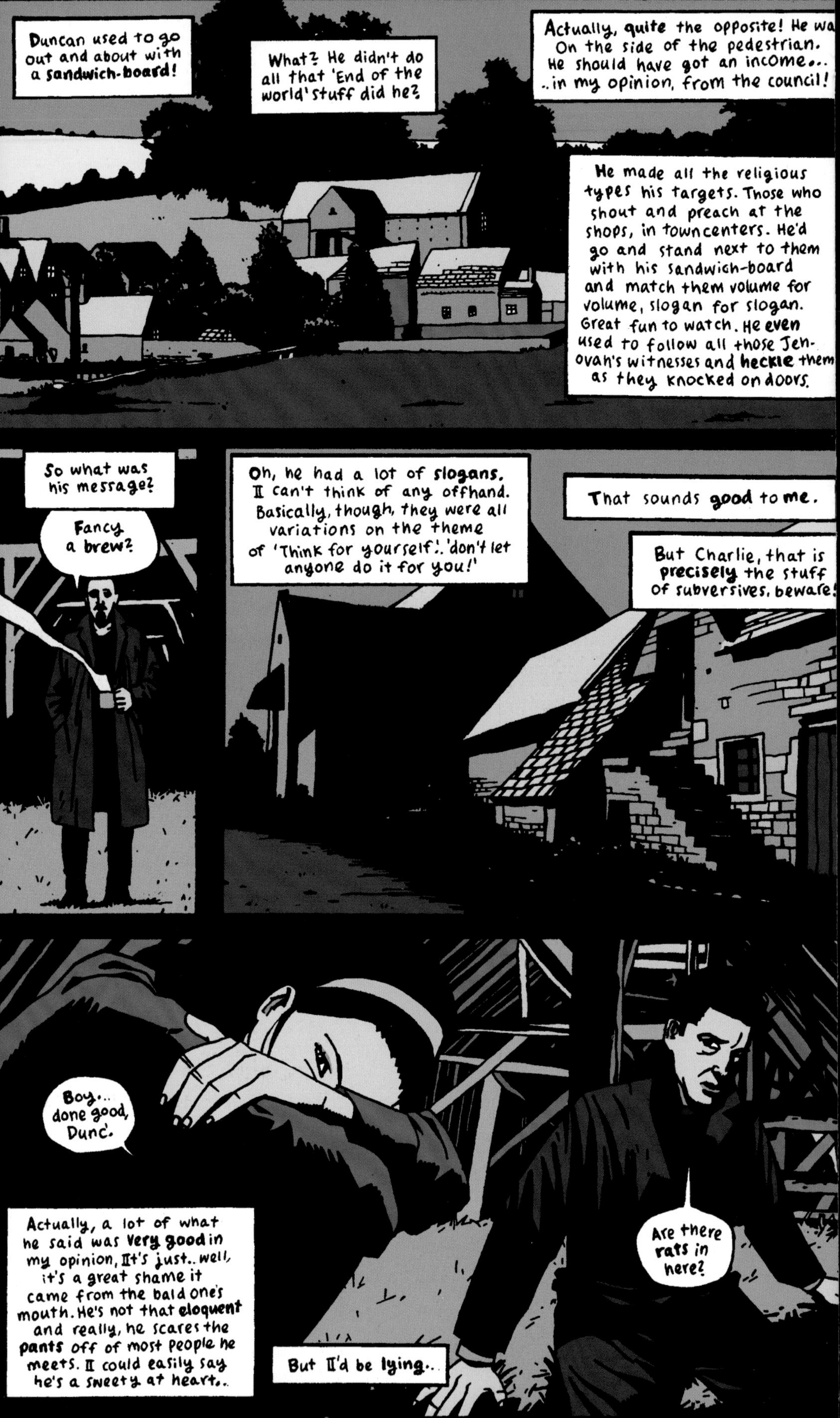

Duncan used to go out and about with a **sandwich-board!**
What? He didn't do all that 'End of the world' stuff did he?
Actually, **quite** the opposite! He wa On the side of the pedestrian. He should have got an income... ..in my opinion, from the council!
He made all the religious types his targets. Those who shout and preach at the shops, in towncenters. He'd go and stand next to them with his sandwich-board and match them volume for volume, slogan for slogan. Great fun to watch. He **even** used to follow all those Jen-ovah's witnesses and **heckle** them as they knocked on doors.
So what was his message?
Fancy a **brew?**
Oh, he had a lot of **slogans.** I can't think of any offhand. Basically, though, they were all variations on the theme of 'Think for yourself'. 'don't let anyone do it for you!'
That sounds **good** to **me.**
But Charlie, that is **precisely** the stuff of subversives, beware!
Boy... done good, Dunc.
Actually, a lot of what he said was **very good** in my opinion, It's just.. well, it's a great shame it came from the bald one's mouth. He's not that **eloquent** and really, he scares the **pants** off of most people he meets. I could easily say he's a sweety at heart..
But I'd be **lying..**
Are there **rats** in here?

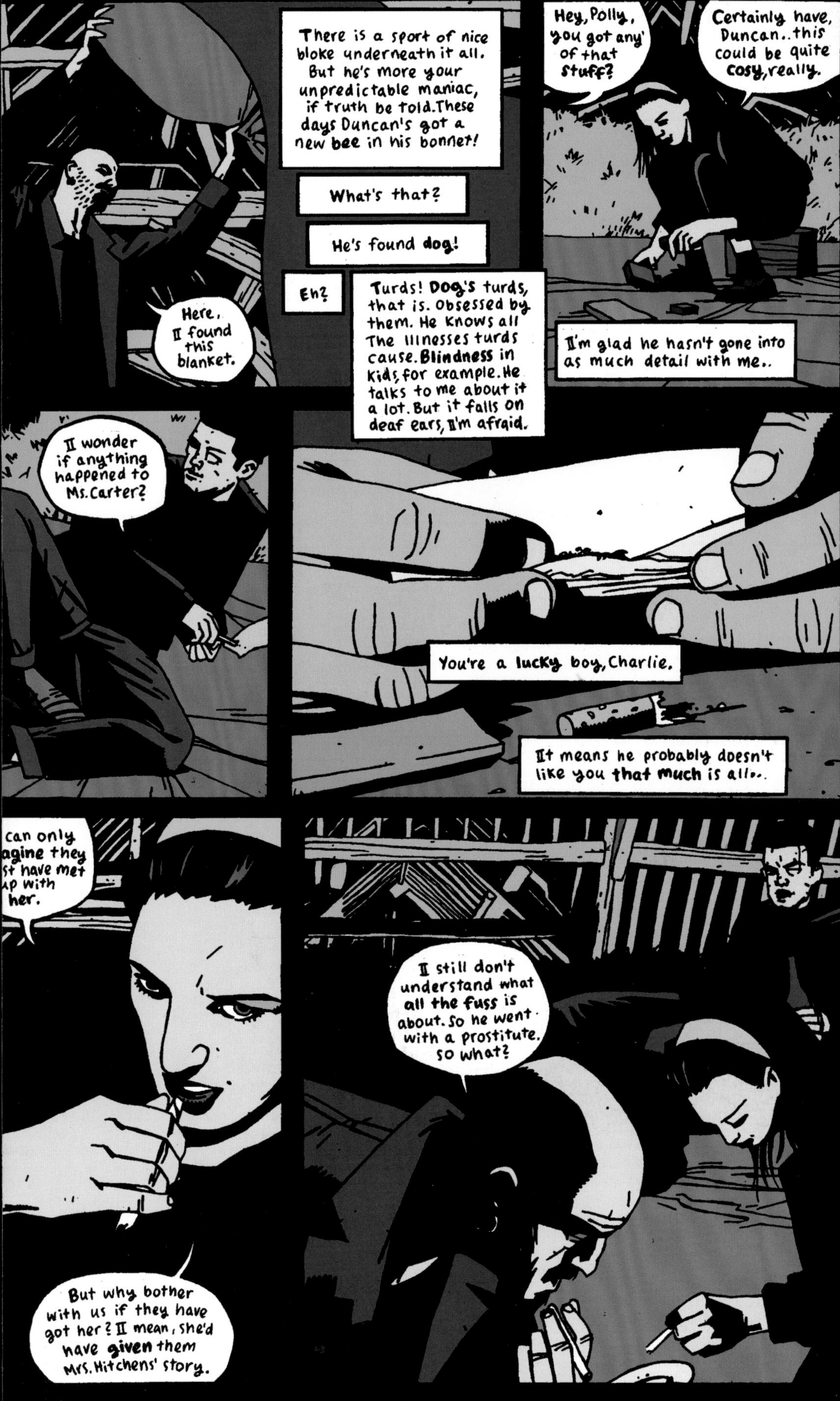

There is a sport of nice bloke underneath it all. But he's more your unpredictable maniac, if truth be told. These days Duncan's got a new bee in his bonnet!
Hey, Polly, you got any' of that stuff?
Certainly have, Duncan.. this could be quite cosy, really.
What's that?
He's found dog!
Eh?
Turds! Dog's turds, that is. Obsessed by them. He knows all The illnesses turds cause. Blindness in kids, for example. He talks to me about it a lot. But it falls on deaf ears, I'm afraid.
Here, I found this blanket.
I'm glad he hasn't gone into as much detail with me..
I wonder if anything happened to Ms. Carter?
You're a lucky boy, Charlie.
It means he probably doesn't like you that much is all..
can only agine they st have met up with her.
I still don't understand what all the fuss is about. So he went with a prostitute. So what?
But why bother with us if they have got her? I mean, she'd have given them Mrs. Hitchens' story.

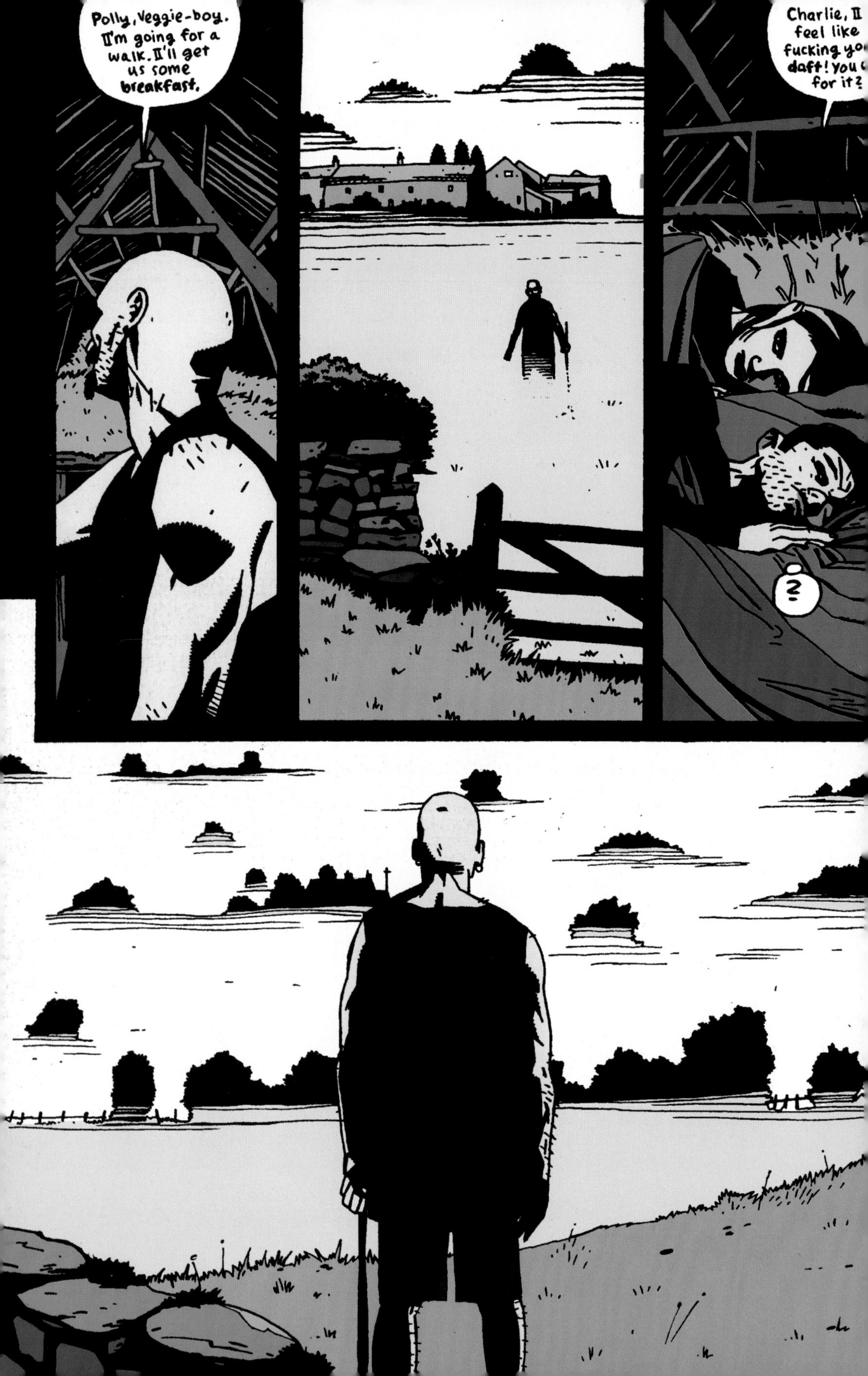

Polly, Veggie-boy. I'm going for a walk. I'll get us some breakfast.
Charlie, I feel like fucking yo daft! You for it?

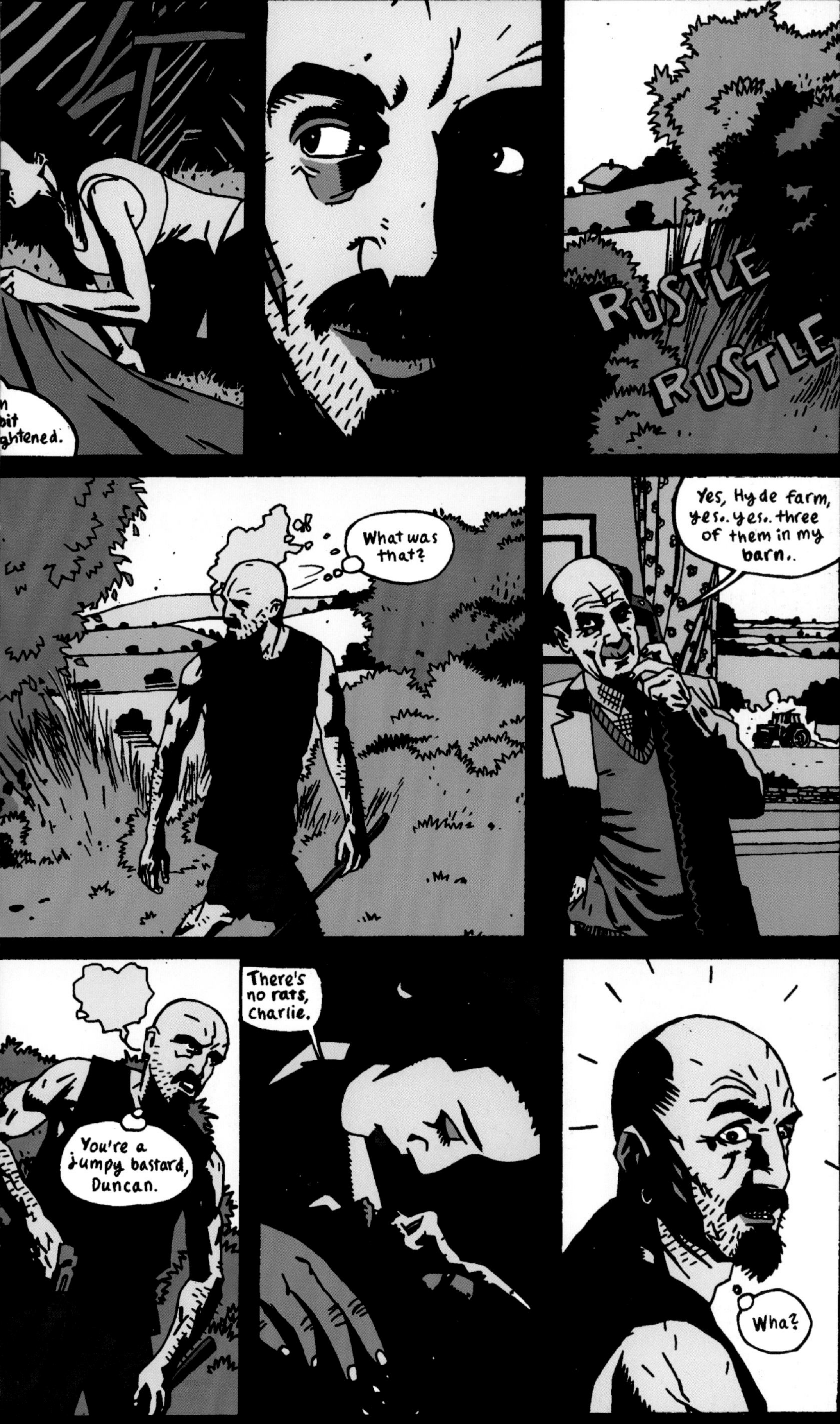
n
bit
ghtened.
RUSTLE
RUSTLE
What was that?
Yes, Hyde farm, yes.. yes.. three of them in my barn..
You're a jumpy bastard, Duncan.
There's no rats, Charlie.
Wha?

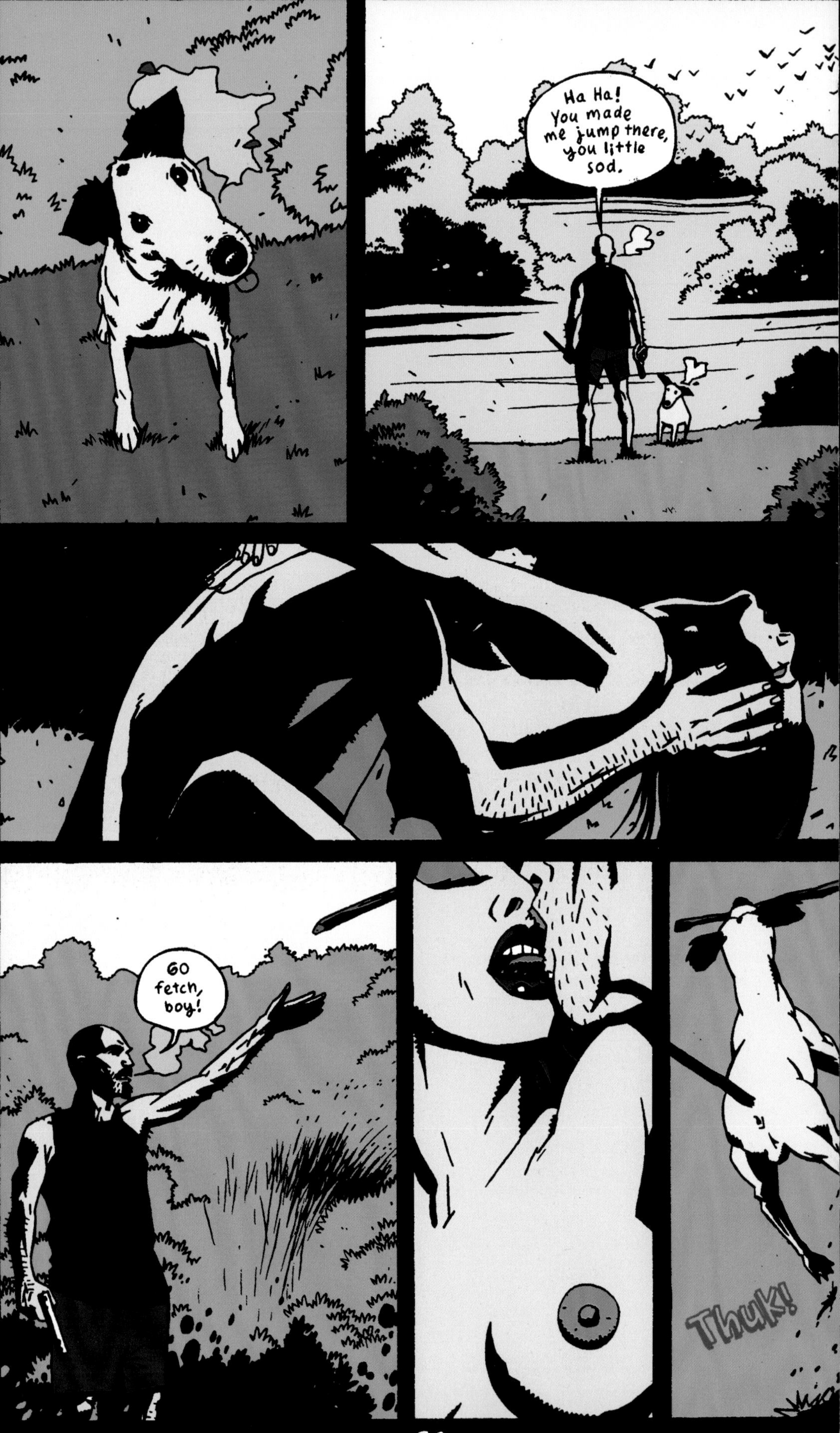
Ha Ha! You made me jump there, you little sod.
GO fetch, boy!
Thuk!

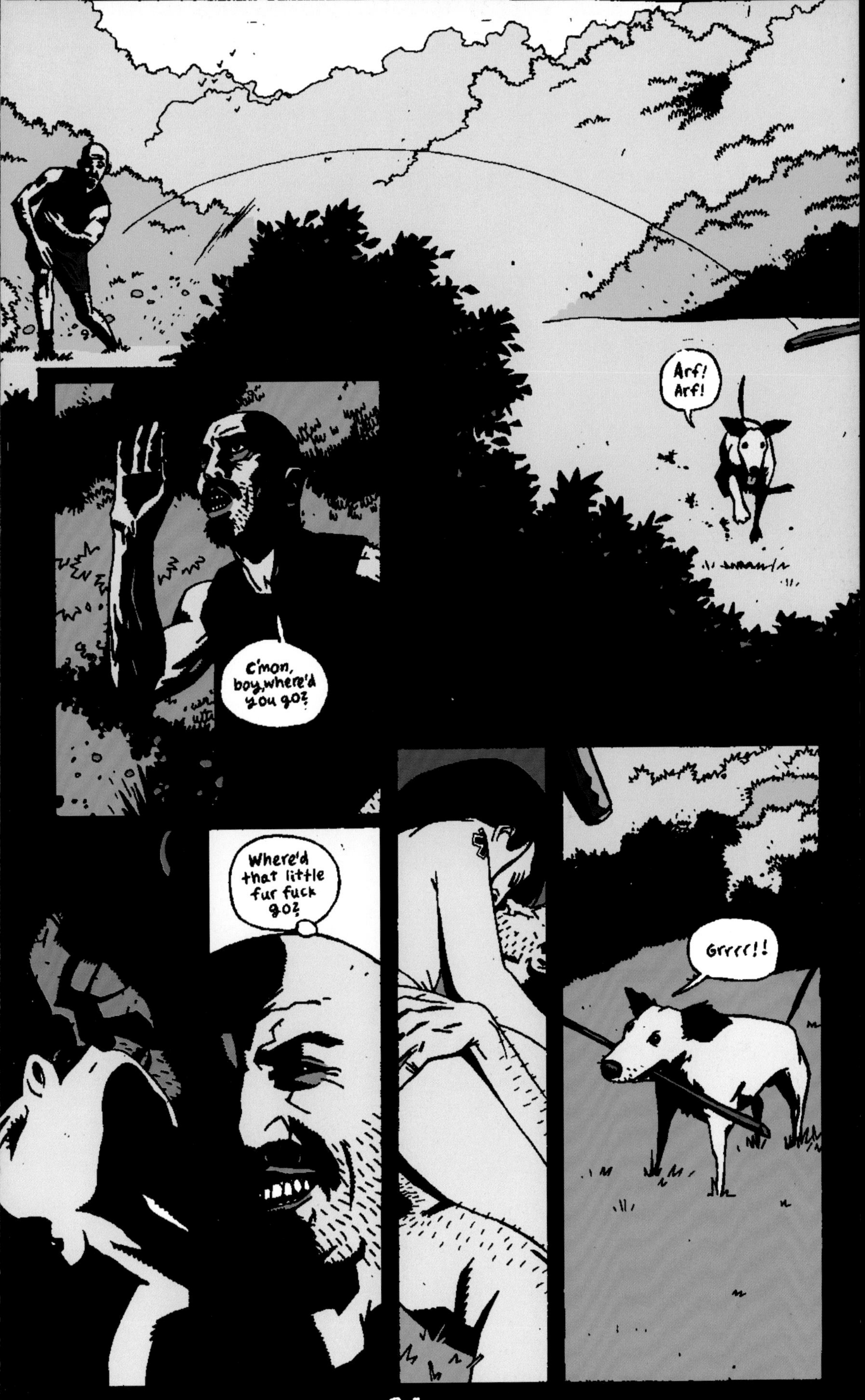
Arf! Arf!
C'mon, boy, where'd you go?
Where'd that little fur fuck go?
Grrrr!!

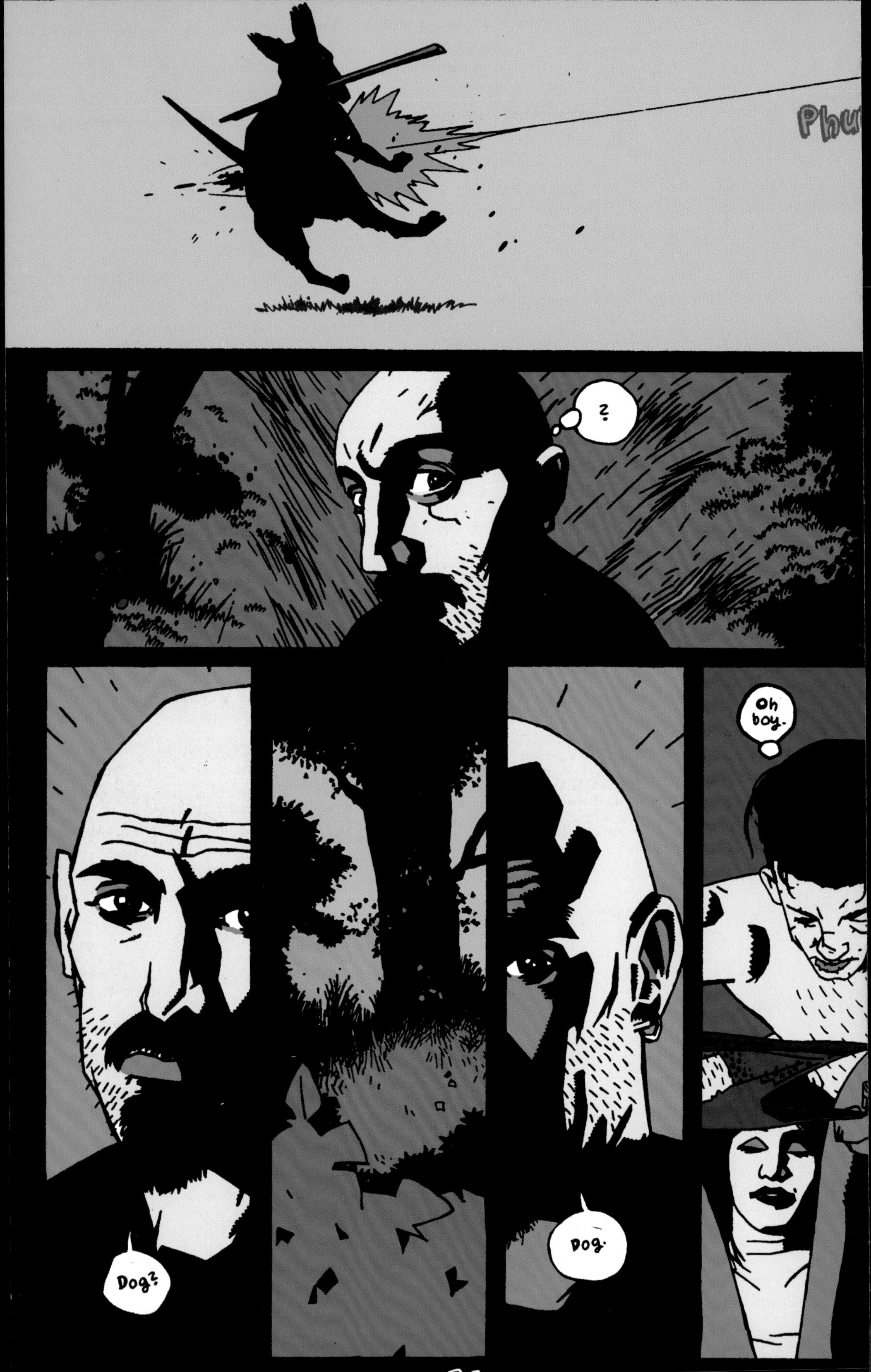
Phu
?
Dog?
Dog.
Oh boy.

He's running. we've **spooked** the suspect..

..East across the field..

d you ow a eal nter on't se his arry?

Get ready, captain.

He'll creep up on it, so the animal is unaware of its impending **doom!**

..If the animal is not frightened, the meat will be **sweet** to taste, if the animal is spooked, the **flesh** is bitter.

The order is, take him out.

When did you last eat natural **sweet meat** from the butcher's?

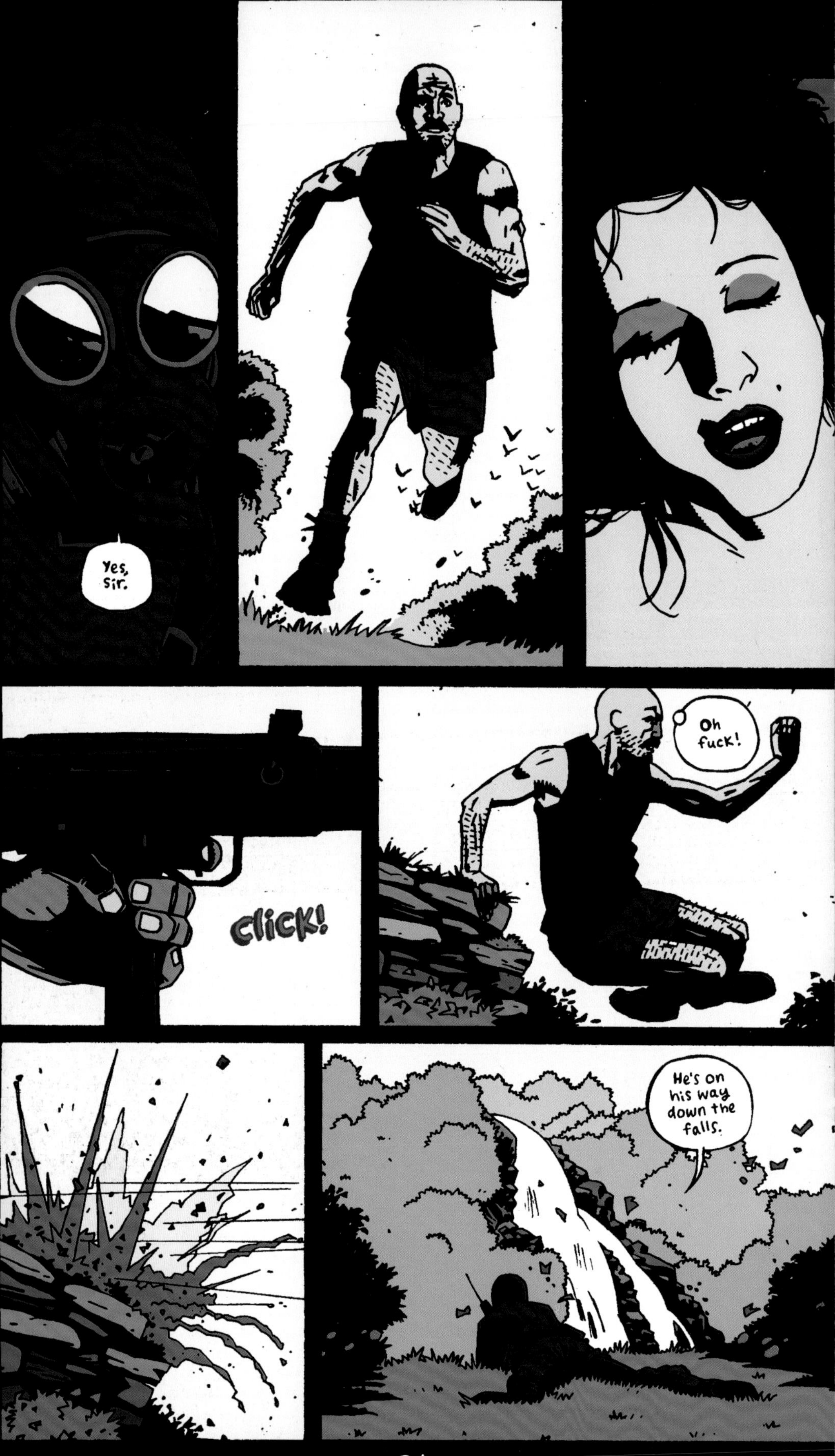
Yes, sir.
CLICK!
Oh fuck!
He's on his way down the falls.

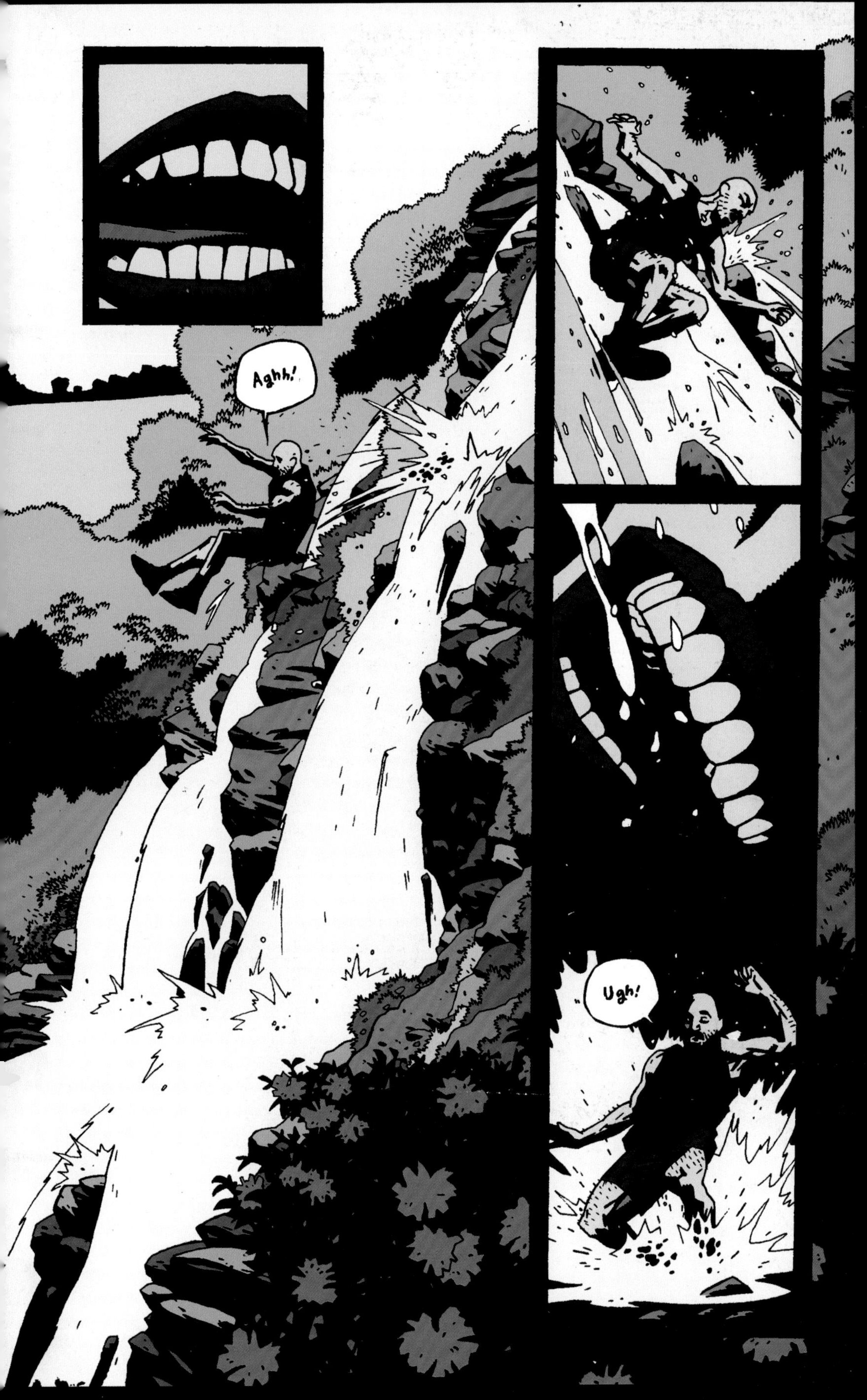
Aghh!
Ugh!

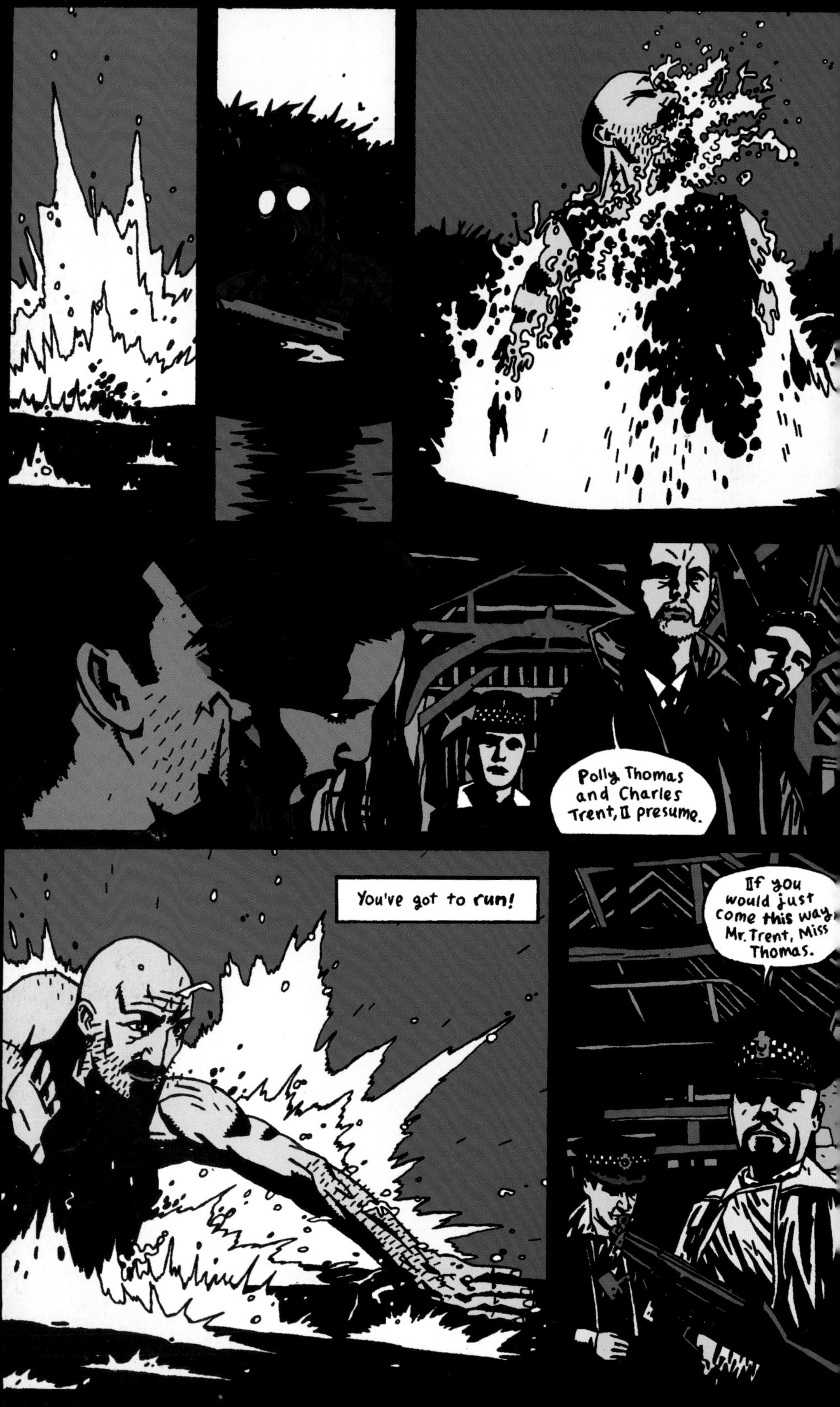
Polly Thomas and Charles Trent, I presume.
You've got to run!
If you would just come this way, Mr. Trent, Miss Thomas.

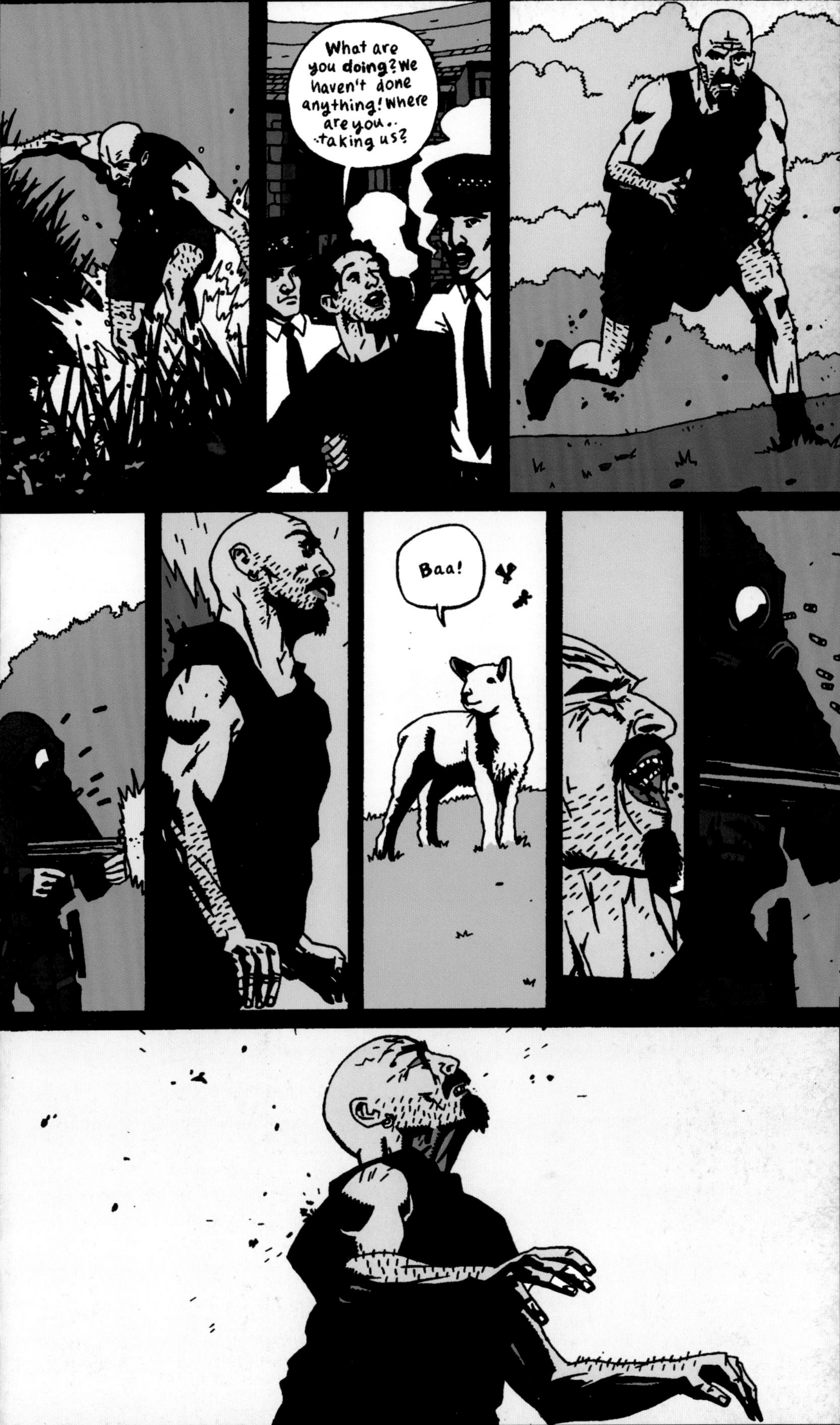
What are you doing? We haven't done anything! Where are you.. ..taking us?
Baa!

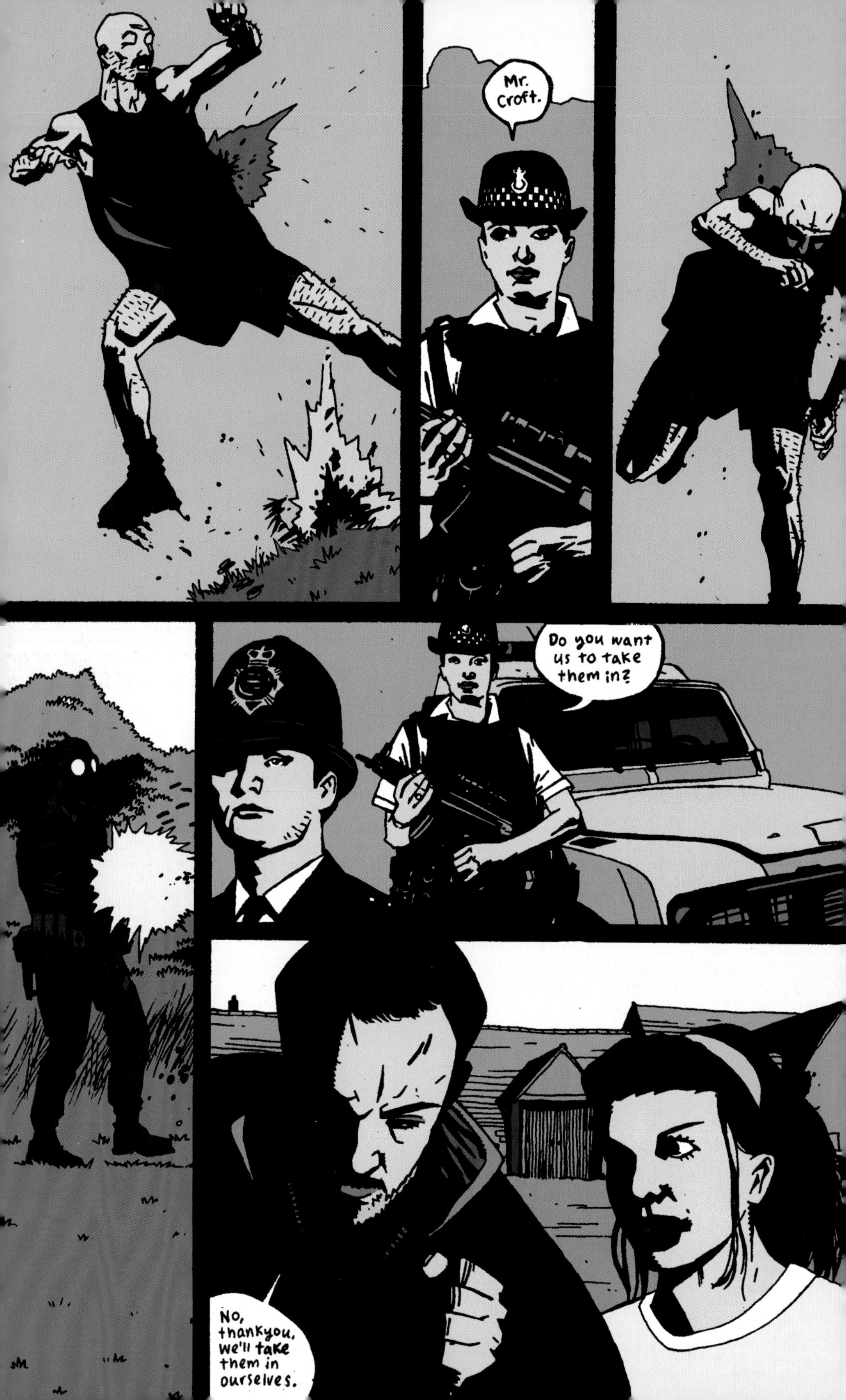
Mr. Croft.
Do you want us to take them in?
No, thankyou, we'll take them in ourselves.

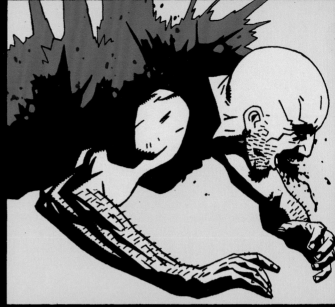

Got to..run.
..to..live!

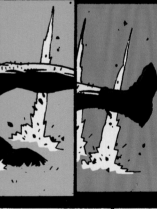

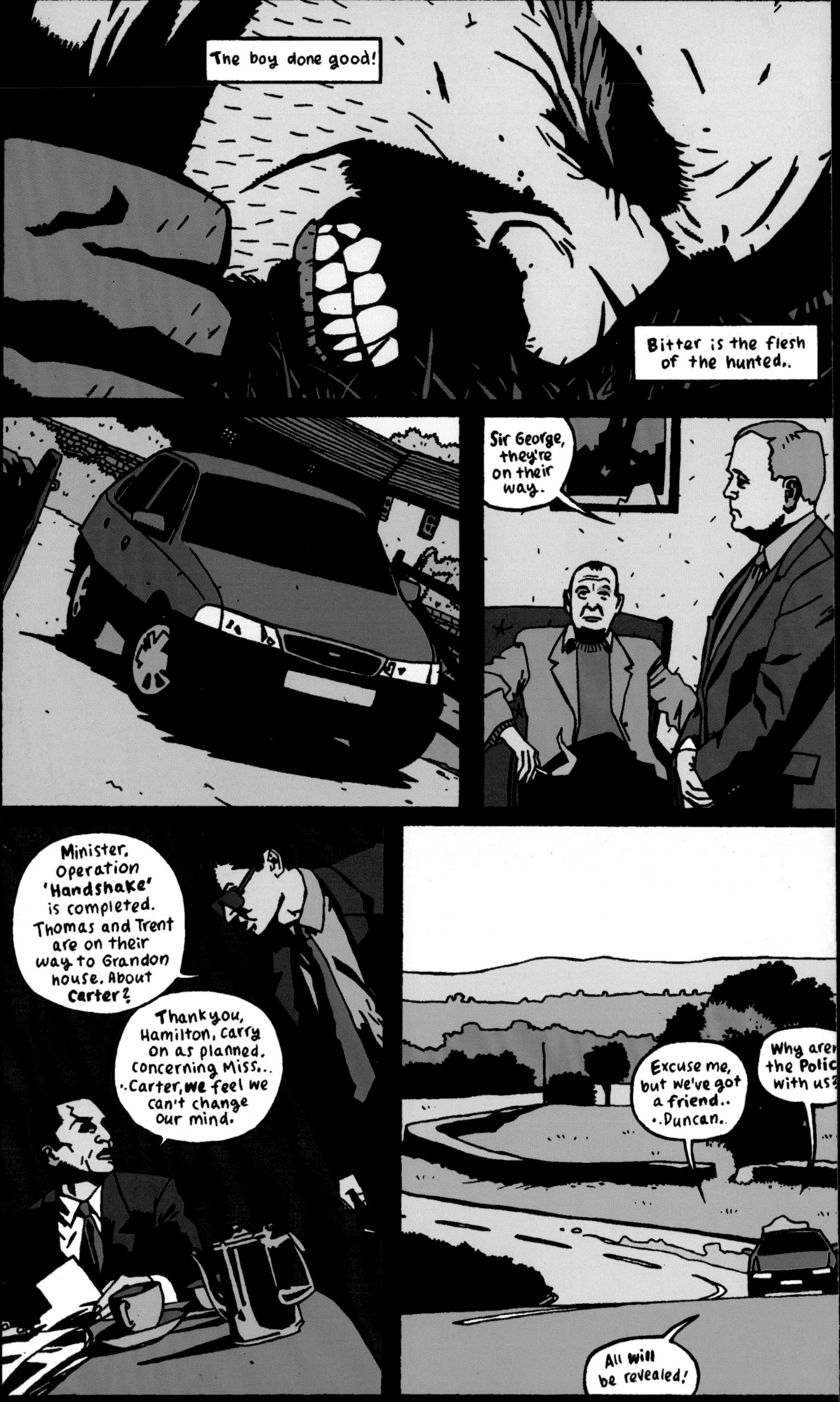
The boy done good!
Bitter is the flesh of the hunted..
Sir George, they're on their way.
Minister, Operation 'Handshake' is completed. Thomas and Trent are on their way to Grandon house. About Carter?
Thankyou, Hamilton, carry on as planned. concerning Miss... ..Carter, we feel we can't change our mind.
Excuse me, but we've got a friend.. ..Duncan..
All will be revealed!

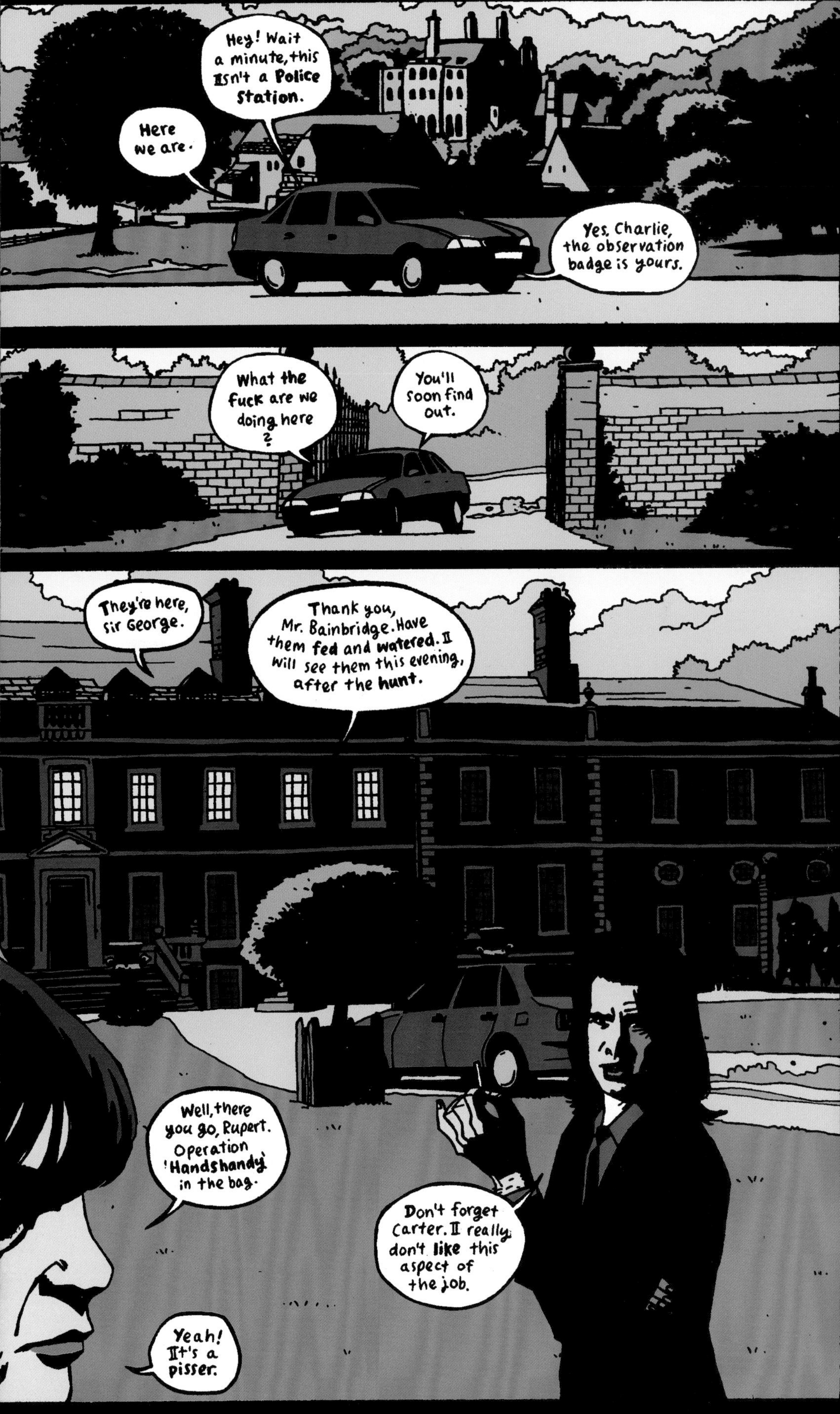
Here we are.
Hey! Wait a minute, this Isn't a Police Station.
Yes, Charlie, the observation badge is yours.
What the fuck are we doing here ?
You'll soon find out.
They're here, sir George.
Thank you, Mr. Bainbridge. Have them fed and watered. I will see them this evening, after the hunt.
Well, there you go, Rupert. Operation 'Handshandy' in the bag.
Don't forget Carter. I really don't like this aspect of the job.
Yeah! It's a pisser.

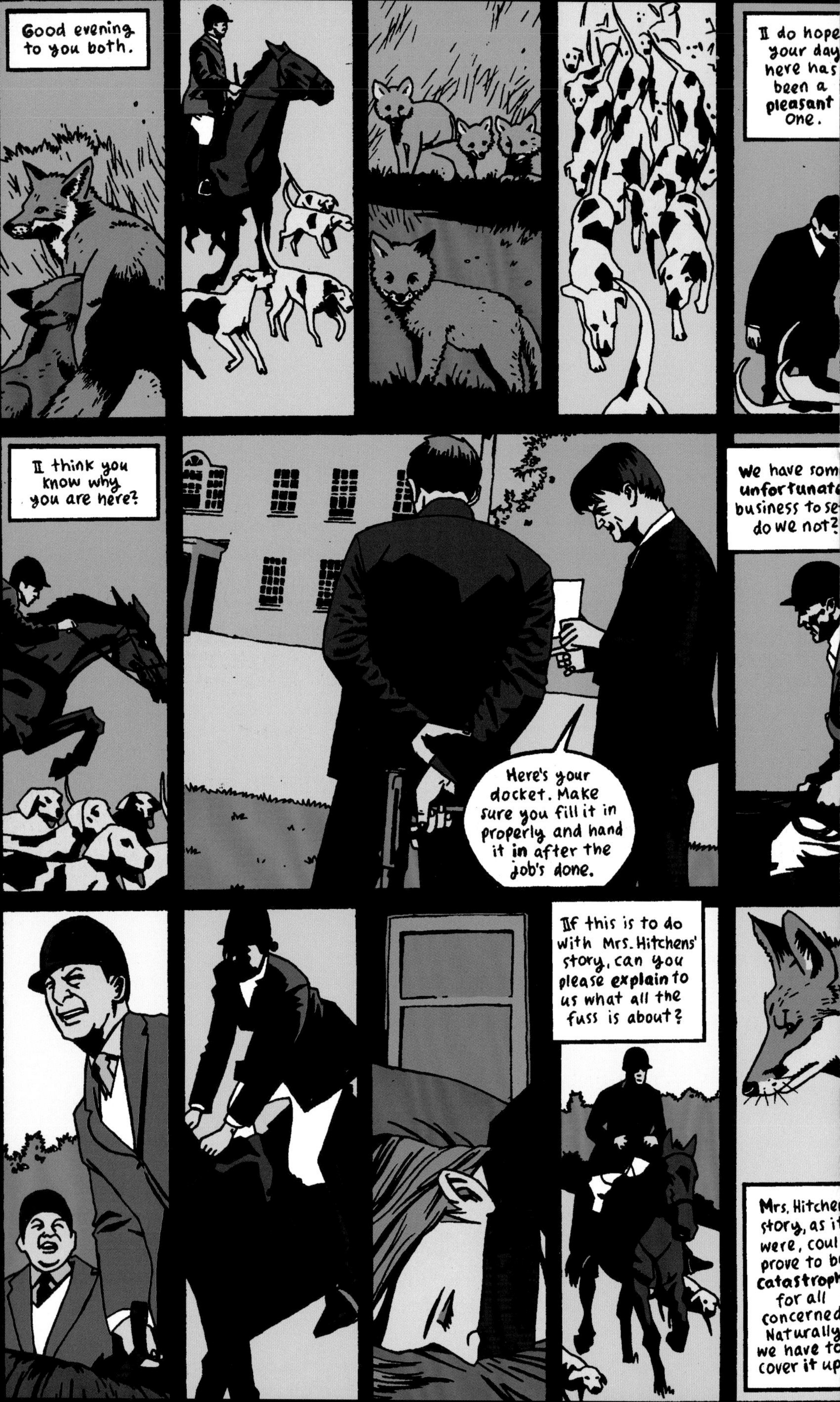
Good evening to you both.
I do hope your day here has been a pleasant one.
I think you know why you are here?
Here's your docket. Make sure you fill it in properly and hand it in after the job's done.
We have some unfortunate business to se do we not?
If this is to do with Mrs. Hitchens' story, can you please explain to us what all the fuss is about?
Mrs. Hitchen story, as it were, coul prove to b catastroph for all concerned Naturally we have to cover it up

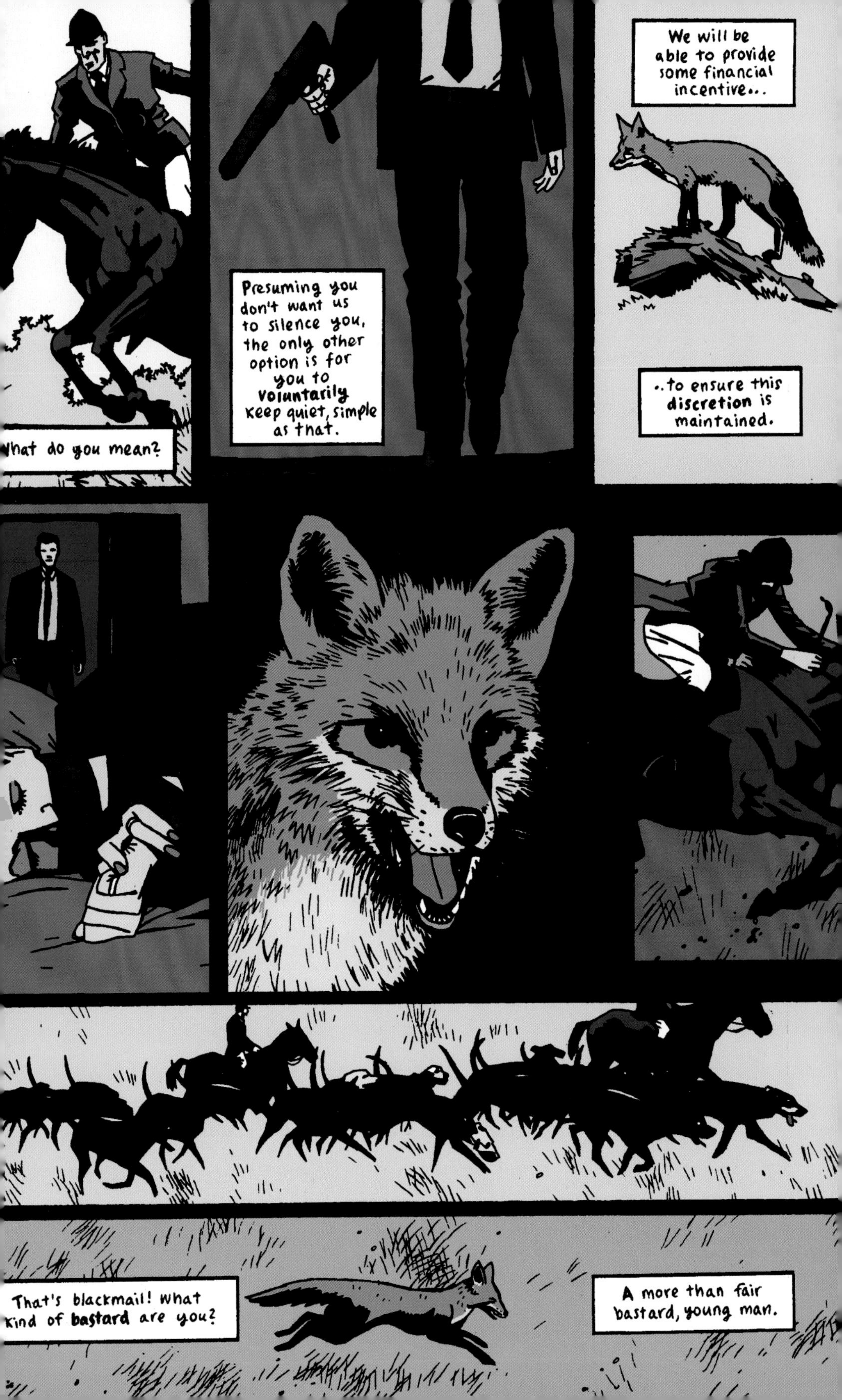
What do you mean?
Presuming you don't want us to silence you, the only other option is for you to voluntarily keep quiet, simple as that.
We will be able to provide some financial incentive...
..to ensure this discretion is maintained.
That's blackmail! What kind of bastard are you?
A more than fair bastard, young man.

It doesn't matter what a man or woman does in life, good or bad...

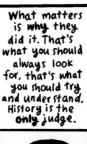

What matters is why they did it. That's what you should always look for, that's what you should try and understand. History is the only judge.

You won't believe me, but I quite like you both. I know you despise me.. If not now, you will eventually I, for that matter, don't really give a **monkey's toss** what you think.

..I really don't.

CLAT!

What are we doing here?

Such is the fate of those who **know** too much. You see, it costs us less to set you two up for life..

..in relative luxury, than it would, and I'll be frank here, to dispose of you.

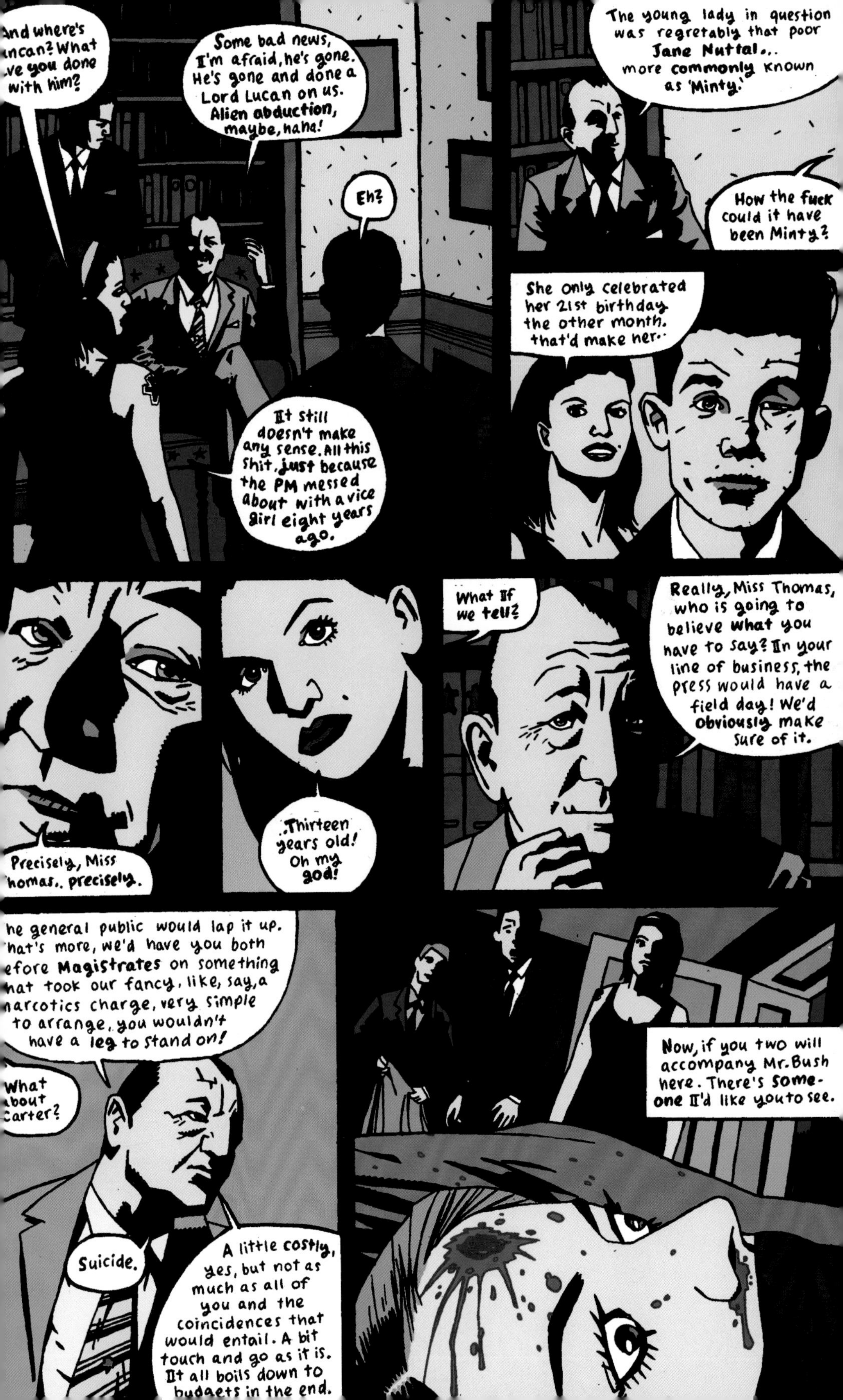
And where's
ucan? What
ve you done
with him?
Some bad news, I'm afraid, he's gone. He's gone and done a Lord Lucan on us. Alien abduction, maybe, haha!
Eh?
It still doesn't make any sense. All this shit, just because the PM messed about with a vice girl eight years ago.
The young lady in question was regretably that poor Jane Nuttal.. more commonly known as 'Minty.'
How the fuck could it have been Minty?
She only celebrated her 21st birthday the other month. that'd make her..
Precisely, Miss
homas.. precisely.
..Thirteen years old! Oh my god!
What If we tell?
Really, Miss Thomas, who is going to believe what you have to say? In your line of business, the press would have a field day! We'd obviously make sure of it.
he general public would lap it up.
hat's more, we'd have you both
efore Magistrates on something
hat took our fancy, like, say, a
narcotics charge, very simple
to arrange. you wouldn't
have a leg to stand on!
What
about
Carter?
Suicide.
A little costly, yes, but not as much as all of you and the coincidences that would entail. A bit touch and go as it is. It all boils down to budgets in the end.
Now, if you two will accompany Mr. Bush here. There's some-one I'd like you to see.

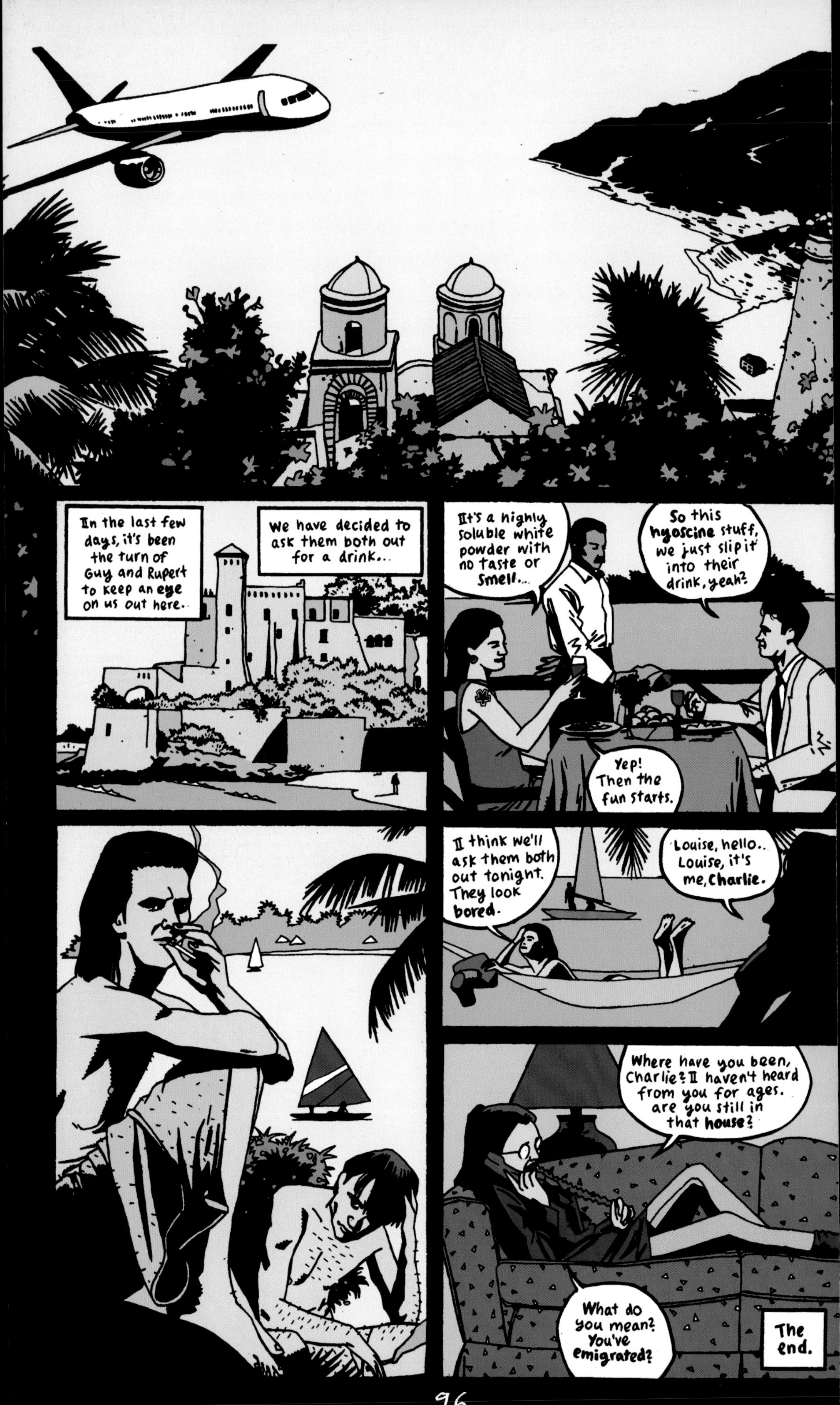

In the last few days, it's been the turn of Guy and Rupert to keep an eye on us out here..
We have decided to ask them both out for a drink...
It's a highly soluble white powder with no taste or smell...
So this hyoscine stuff, we just slip it into their drink, yeah?
Yep! Then the fun starts.
I think we'll ask them both out tonight. They look bored.
Louise, hello.. Louise, it's me, Charlie.
Where have you been, Charlie? I haven't heard from you for ages. are you still in that house?
What do you mean? You've emigrated?
The end.

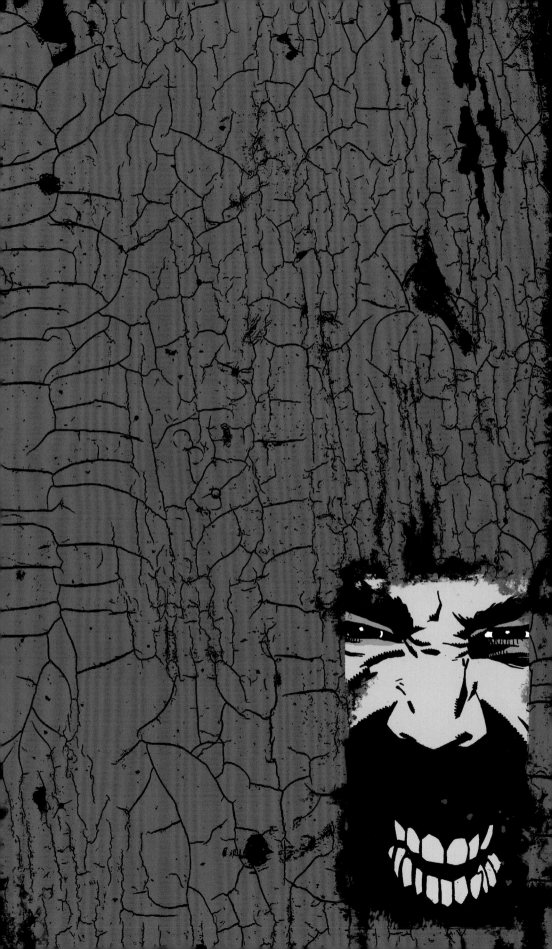

Bal Speer

Has been married for nearly twenty
fun-packed years and has two great
children. He lives in a village in
Wiltshire, England, and lectures part-
time in Narrative and Sequential Art.
He has been a freelance illustrator
for twelve years. Before that he
worked in animation, where he met
Moebius, who informed him that there
was no future in graphic novels and
consistently beat him at table tennis.
He has a passion for music, books,
films, photography, occulture, pubs,
camping, Guernsey jumpers, psychology
and beer. Most of all, he loves spending
time with his family and his
wonderful gang of friends.

Special Thanks

To Nick Cave
and Mark E. Smith
and the late John Peel

Thanks also to

Tracey Rogers,

Thomas Ravenscroft,

Suzi Goodrich,

Dave Marlow,

Pete Smart,

Pete Field,

festival Michael,

Mike the hairdresser,

and Dorothy Howe.

Written and Illustrated by

Bal Speer

Rebecca Taylor, Editor
Howling Monkey Studio, Design
Scott Newman, Production Manager
Creator photograph provided by Peter Smart

Archaia Entertainment LLC

PJ Bickett, CEO
Mark Smylie, CCO
Mike Kennedy, Publisher
Stephen Christy, Editor-in-Chief

Published by Archaia

Archaia Entertainment LLC
1680 Vine Street, Suite 1010
Los Angeles, CA, 90028 USA
www.archaia.com

ARCHAIA™
NEW STORIES. NEW WORLDS.

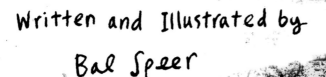

BLACK CHARITY
January 2012
FIRST PRINTING

10 9 8 7 6 5 4 3 2 1

ISBN: 1-936393-29-8
ISBN-13: 978-1-936393-29-9

PRINTED IN CHINA BY GLOBAL PSD.